WAS NEVER ALONE

Nidia Díaz

I WAS NEVER ALONE

A prison diary from El Salvador

OCEAN

The publisher gratefully acknowledges the assistance of Genevieve Vaughan, Carmen Medina, Jorge Timossi, Diane Atkinson, Rosemary Evans and Lisa Shnookal.

Cover design by David Spratt

ISBN paper 1 875284 13 3
ISBN cloth 1 875284 14 1

First edition, 1992

Published by Ocean Press,
GPO Box 3279GG, Melbourne, Victoria 3001, Australia

Distributed in the USA by The Talman Company,
150 Fifth Avenue, New York, NY 10011, USA

Distributed in Britain and Europe by Central Books,
99 Wallis Road, London E9 5LN, Britain

Distributed in Southern Africa by Grassroots Books,
PO Box A267, Avondale, Harare, Zimbabwe

Distributed in Australia by Astam Books,
162-8 Parramatta Road, Stanmore, NSW 2048, Australia

Printed by Australian Print Group, Maryborough, Vic.

Contents

To the Farabundo Martí National Liberation Front.

To all those *compañeros*
who did not get the chance
that I had.

To Alejandro,
my little one so shaken by the war,
the complement to my life.

María Marta Valladares
(Nidia Díaz)

María Marta Valladares, known as Nidia Díaz, is a leading member of the Farabundo Martí National Liberation Front (FMLN).

Born on November 14, 1952, in San Salvador, she was the third of four children.

Her activity as a fighter for social justice commenced at the age of thirteen when she participated in pastoral and literacy campaigns sponsored by social and Christian organizations.

In 1971, at eighteen years of age, she became active in political struggle and by 1975 was part of the leadership of the Salvadoran revolutionary movement. During this time she completed four years study of psychology.

From 1981 until 1983 she was part of the urban underground leadership of the FMLN. As part of the FDR-FMLN delegation she participated in the negotiations with the Duarte government at La Palma in October 1984.

On April 18, 1985, she was seriously wounded in combat with four bullet wounds and burns to her body. She was captured by a U.S. military adviser. Taking part in the capture was Félix Rodríguez, a CIA agent working for Oliver North in El Salvador. For four days her capture was not acknowledged by the Salvadoran Armed Forces. She was interrogated without interruption for sixteen days and subsequently held in solitary confinement for six months in the National Police Headquarters.

On October 24, 1985, she was released with other political prisoners in exchange for the daughter of President Duarte.

In April 1987 she was named president of the "Mélida Anaya Montes" Salvadoran Union for Women's Liberation. She was appointed to the Political-Diplomatic Commission of the FMLN in May 1987 and in August of that year was named director of the FMLN's Commission for the Protection and Promotion of Human Rights.

In October 1989 she became part of the FMLN delegation in

1

talks with the Cristiani government. She is a member of the FMLN delegation for the UN-sponsored negotiations initiated in Geneva on April 4, 1990. She has continued in this role through 1991.

She is the mother of a son.

Preface

"In prison everything is intended to make you feel alone, isolated, defeated. Your captors say over and over: 'We are your father, your brother, your family. No one else cares about you.' If for a moment you believe them, and forget that your people and the struggle still exist, then you are truly alone.

"Alone, isolated in a prison cell, blindfolded and tortured, you must always remember you are never really alone, that your people are there beside you and there is always hope. Then the moral victory is yours."

This is how Nidia Díaz recalled the experience of her imprisonment after she was wounded and captured in combat by a U.S. adviser in El Salvador in April 1985.

To recall those 190 days of prison, torture, and interrogation was not easy. Yet Nidia felt it was her duty to remember, to recount to others how it is that people survive the prisons of El Salvador. She also felt a responsibility to present her testimony to the international solidarity movement, which had played a part in her eventual release.

In contrast to the humility of *I was never alone*, the CIA agent Felix Rodríguez, alias Max Gomez, is eager to boast about his role in the capture of the guerrilla commander, Nidia Díaz. Rodríguez, a Cuban-American, in his book *Shadow Warrior: The CIA hero of a hundred unknown battles* (1989) also gives details of his part in the capture of Che Guevara in Bolivia in 1967. In an interview with the *Miami Herald* (October 16, 1989) Rodríguez described his personal museum of "war trophies" which includes Che Guevara's pipe and Nidia Díaz's bra.

Rodríguez's testimony exposes the active role of U.S. military "advisers" in Central America. He describes himself as directly responsible to Colonel Oliver North, one of the key players in the Iran-Contragate scandal – the full details of which have yet to be revealed.

Nidia Díaz survived to tell her story because her capture coincided with President Duarte's need to show the U.S. Congress that human rights were respected under the new government in El Salvador. Yet, although she was seriously wounded at the time of her capture, with bad burns and numerous fractures and bullet wounds, she had to endure four months of terrible pain before an operation was performed. During the first few days of her imprisonment and interrogation she was not even given as much as an aspirin to alleviate her agony. Unable to walk or even sit properly in a chair, she was carried about from one interrogation session to the next on a mattress.

The capture of Nidia Díaz and the extraordinary circumstances of her release in exchange for President Duarte's daughter Inés attracted international attention. While in prison Nidia was visited by several U.S. congressmen and conducted many interviews with the foreign media, including two interviews for CBS television. When Duarte visited the United States in 1985 he was confronted by human rights groups demanding that Nidia be allowed the operation she urgently required.

El Salvador is still a country at war. This has been clearly recognized by the United Nations in sponsoring peace talks between the Cristiani government[1] and the Farabundo Martí National Liberation Front (FMLN). Nidia Díaz has been part of the FMLN negotiating team in these talks.

In an interview with the publishers in May 1991, she briefly outlined the background to the struggle in El Salvador:

"The movement in El Salvador dates back to 1970 when the political-military struggle began in response to a contraction of democratic rights. In 1975 there were five revolutionary organizations. These organizations were the People's Liberation Front (FPL), the People's Revolutionary Army (ERP), the Central American Worker's Revolutionary Party (PRTC), the National Resistance (RN), and the Communist Party of El Salvador (PC).

"By the end of the 1970s these revolutionary forces had realized that none of them alone could lead the popular struggle that was developing. The FMLN was therefore founded on October 10, 1980. At the end of that year the FMLN formed an alliance with the Democratic Revolutionary Front (FDR) which included the

---

1. Alfredo Cristiani was elected president of El Salvador in 1989 as the candidate of ARENA (Nationalist Republican Alliance).

Social Democrats and Christian Socialists in order to lead the 1981 offensive.

"Salvadorans have been fighting military dictatorship and economic injustice for sixty years. The ruling families, often referred to as the oligarchy, own most of the land, but represent only 0.4 percent of the population. Coffee has been the main source of their wealth. This oligarchy became more and more dependent on the military after the 1932 insurrection during which 30,000 workers and peasants were killed.

"Farabundo Martí was a teacher, a worker, a man of the people, who founded the Communist Party of El Salvador in the early 1930s. He led the insurrection of 1932 at the time of a great crisis in the coffee industry and massive unemployment. Unemployed rural workers were the heart of the 1932 uprising. Martí was captured and executed. But the principles of social justice and democracy he fought for are represented in the FMLN today.

"The Salvadoran Armed Forces have assumed greater and greater power as civilian governments have come and gone. There have been various elections over the years, but in our view, as long as there are no truly democratic conditions allowing a free, representative system for the whole nation, and opportunities for all to participate, such elections cannot express the nation's wishes. Fair and democratic elections cannot take place in a state of siege, in a state of war.

"After the murder of Archbishop Romero in 1980 while conducting mass in the cathedral, it was clear that the armed struggle was the only possible course for political and social change. That is how the guerrilla movement became generalized. It was obvious that the oligarchy would never willingly accept the sharing of political, economic, and military power. The guerrilla struggle was therefore a course of action forced on to us. For ten years now we have been preparing the people to defend themselves against repression and massacres by the military. Archbishop Romero's assassination showed the world that absolutely nobody is safe in El Salvador.

"Thus we ourselves are a product of dictatorship. We did not start militarism in El Salvador, but rather represent the reponse to that militarism. The workers had to create their own revolutionary army.

"Since 1981 70,000 Salvadorans have died in the civil war. A further 7,000 have disappeared and thousands have been imprisoned and tortured. There are still about 400 political prisoners in El Salvador.

"For a long time the Salvadoran government used the peace negotiations with the FMLN as a tactical game to appease the United States Congress. The first negotiations were held in La Palma in 1984[1]. The military resisted these steps towards a dialogue still believing in the possibility of inflicting a military defeat on the FMLN.

"It was only after the FMLN conducted a major military offensive against the regime in 1989 that the negotiations were taken more seriously and the United Nations became involved.

"Since April 1990 the UN has sponsored the negotiations giving both sides the same rights. We are progressing slowly, despite all the obstacles put in our way. We believe there is no going back on this path of negotiation.

"On the other hand, United States aid has been the most important factor in prolonging the Salvadoran conflict. The U.S. military training and aid constitute interference in our country. Salvadorans should solve our own problems, decide our own future.

"The war in El Salvador has not been imported from abroad. It is the result of our country's economic, political, and social situation. It is the response to successive military dictatorships, the banning of political parties, and the blatant social and economic injustice. Throughout history our people have fought a patriotic struggle for independence and social justice, like that led by Farabundo Martí."

It was during her period of convalescence abroad, whilst undergoing grueling physiotherapy that Nidia wrote *I was never alone*. Somewhere between accepting and rejecting her responsibility to recall, between carefully recording her experience and throwing down the microphone, typing and pounding on the typewriter, Nidia wrote these pages. It was "a very difficult birth," she says, and she is not entirely satisfied with the "baby":

1. Nidia Díaz participated as one of the FMLN representatives in these negotiations in La Palma in October 1984.

"I am told that the book is more a reflection of my revolutionary ideology than of my own personal emotions. But in prison there's no choice — if you do not hang on to your convictions, your ideology, you are lost. You cannot reveal the slightest personal feeling to your captors, to your interrogators. This was something I had to try hard not to do. Later, when I started to write, it just flowed in the same way. I felt the same constraint. This is how I survived in prison minute by minute — holding on, resisting."

Originally published in El Salvador in 1988 and subsequently throughout Latin America, this English language edition of *I was never alone* exposes the brutality suffered not only by Nidia Diaz but the hundreds of Salvadorans who remain political prisoners. It also helps explain the history of the popular struggle in El Salvador today.

Along with the reflections on her family, her *compañeros*, and her people, Nidia presents an insight into the personalities of various Salvadoran political figures. Her book also highlights the invaluable work of the Salvadoran Church throughout these years of civil war.

I was never alone is therefore much more than a moving personal testimony of a political prisoner. It is a tribute to the spirit and courage of Salvadoran women, the Farabundo Martís of the Third World, and fighters for social justice everywhere.

Deborah Shnookal

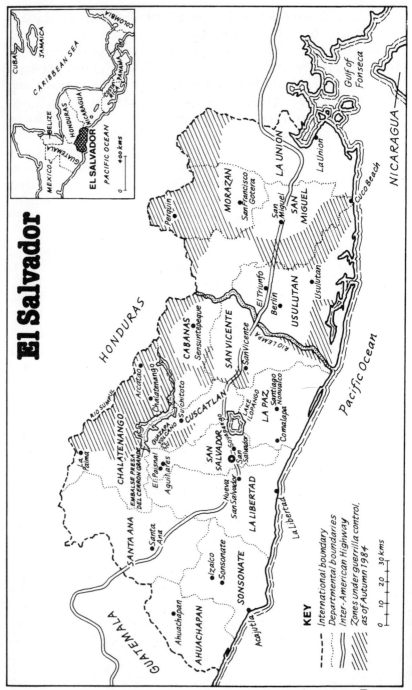

El Salvador

Latin American Bureau

KEY

- – – – International boundary
- ⋯⋯⋯ Departmental boundaries
- ═══ Inter-American Highway
- ▨ Zones under guerrilla control, as of Autumn 1984

0 10 20 30 kms

Inset map labels:

CUBA
JAMAICA
CARIBBEAN SEA
COLOMBIA
PANAMA
COSTA RICA
NICARAGUA
HONDURAS
EL SALVADOR
GUATEMALA
BELIZE
MEXICO
PACIFIC OCEAN
0   400 kms

Main map labels:

GUATEMALA
HONDURAS
NICARAGUA
Pacific Ocean
Gulf of Fonseca

AHUACHAPAN
Ahuachapan
SONSONATE
Sonsonate
Izalco
Nueva San Salvador
Acajutla
SANTA ANA
Santa Ana
LA LIBERTAD
La Libertad
SAN SALVADOR
San Salvador
LA PAZ
Santiago Nonualco
Comalapa
Lake Ilopango
CUSCATLAN
Suchitoto
Guazapa Volcano
Aguilares
El Paisnal
I.A. Palma
CHALATENANGO
EMBALSE PRESA DEL CERRON GRANDE
Chalatenango
Arcatao
RIO SUMPUL
CABANAS
Sensuntepeque
SAN VICENTE
San Vicente
El Triunfo
Berlin
RIO LEMPA
USULUTAN
Usulutan
MORAZAN
Perquin
San Francisco Gotera
SAN MIGUEL
San Miguel
LA UNION
La Union
Cuco Beach

Introduction

As the reader of this new edition of *I was never alone* delves more deeply into the book and reacts to the profoundly humanistic and revolutionary feelings shown in the testimony of Nidia Díaz, they will have to do something else too: they will have to add to what has already been written the numerous new events which have followed this story.

One tragic and revealing incident which can never be forgotten is the savage and cowardly murder of six Jesuit priests and two of their employees by Salvadoran government police on November 16, 1989. Among the victims were Ignacio Ellacuría and Ignacio Martín Baro, who played an important part in the publication of the first edition of this book. Their murder shows clearly that the government's death squads are continuing their appalling crimes, and that they remain an important and integral part of the Armed Forces.

These death squads have never disappeared from the Salvadoran political scene. For many high-ranking army officers the victory at the polls in March 1989 of Roberto D'Aubuisson's ARENA party – the accused and proved planner of Archbishop Romero's assassination in 1980 – means returning to their "finest" days of the dirty war of 1979-81.

This atrocious crime, and the following parody of a trial of six officers including a colonel, highlights that the new president, Alfredo Cristiani, and the Salvadoran legal system are an apparently legitimate screen to hide those who really hold power in El Salvador: the military dictatorship and an unscrupulous economic oligarchy. They are powers that exist thanks solely to the support and financial aid given by successive governments of the United States.

We can state with absolute certainty – however much they may deny it and speak of respect for human rights and defending democracy – that the U.S. government's policy of financial and political support for the Salvadoran regime and Armed Forces means sponsoring and guaranteeing the continuation of the death squads. In the same way, the Salvadoran people are denied their right to democracy. It is U.S. policy which supports the ever-increasing militarization of political life in El Salvador and which is transforming the government's army into a superpower.

Indeed, history shows that democracy in Central America has always been a parody. Today in El Salvador, thanks to over $4 billion handed over by Presidents Reagan and Bush, the situation is worse than ever.

The reader should also study this testimony in the light of new proofs of the military strength and vitality of the guerrilla army of the Farabundo Martí National Liberation Front. The offensive of November 1989 contradicted all the predictions of the Salvadoran and U.S. governments about the "weakened social base" of the revolutionary forces, and gave lie to the Army High Command, which had spoken about a considerable decrease in guerrilla forces. They had said that most of the guerrilla forces were "under control" in their traditional "sanctuaries" within the mountainous regions of the country.

On the night of November 11, in a simultaneous attack which made a mockery of the government's military control, over 6,000 guerrilla fighters stormed the centers of the four main cities in the country. Two thousand of them entered the capital San Salvador. This was no mere flash in the pan. The *guerrilleros* fought in those cities all the rest of November.

Carrying out an offensive of this size presupposes the active participation of no less than 20,000 revolutionaries. Hundreds are dedicated to secret logistic work while many thousands to exploratory assignments and practical support. Thousands of troops had to be moved over a period of two months. The expensive military intelligence of the United States was shown to be of little practical value. This surprise offensive was tremendously effective.

So great was popular support of the guerrilla offensive that there was a possibility that it might all become a real people's uprising. The government decided to crush any such attempt. On November 13 they put into action the "Jakarta" plan and aerial attacks with bombardments and rockets were launched on the poorer urban areas. Thirty thousand homes of the poor were destroyed, an unknown number of civilians killed (among them the six Jesuit priests and their employees), and over 6,000 arrests during the week November 13-20, 1989. To be young, to live in a poor suburb, or to be a member of a trade union was reason enough to be imprisoned.

In the midst of the Government's desperation, the FMLN occupied the most exclusive districts of the capital, took over the El Salvador Sheraton Hotel, and a group of U.S. military advisers were surrounded. The secretary general of the Organization of American States (OAS) was also in the hotel at the time and the FMLN negotiated the evacuation from the hotel of all these and other guests. The FMLN demonstrated its military efficiency and its coordination of the guerrilla units. Their behavior was the same in all activity carried out, whether in exclusive suburbs or poorer districts. The behavior of government troops was completely different – they shot anything that moved, sacked houses, showed no respect for civilians, murdered the wounded, and displayed incredible brutality towards the bodies of guerrilla fighters killed in combat, whose ears they cut off to provide evidence to the U.S. military of their own "heroic exploits."

Two things, therefore, stood out during the offensive of November 1989: first, the military strength of the FMLN – based on its deep-rooted influence among the masses – and the exceptional military professionalism of the guerrilla troops. Second, the brutality of the government soldiers, their officers' unscrupulousness, and the cruelty they used to compensate for their inability to hang on to power by legitimate political and military means. These differences between the two forces could be neither hidden nor reversed. This reaffirms the view that there is only one sensible and realistic way out of the political situation and the war being suffered in El Salvador: a negotiated solution.

The beginning of the negotiating process through the offices of the secretary general of the United Nations is an event without precedence – the greatest opportunity of establishing both national reconciliation in our country and a truly democratic government.

For such a solution it is essential that an agreement is reached by all four sectors – the FMLN, the Salvadoran government, political parties, and social forces. This will be possible only on the basis of political agreement guaranteeing real democracy. To this end, the nation must be demilitarized. This can only be achieved by ending the impunity of the regime's army: it must be purged, and changed into an organization answerable to civil authority. It must cease to be the superpower it is at present, thanks to the multibillion dollar aid given by the U.S. government.

The FMLN is fighting for such a true democracy, based on a strategic principle: complete democracy in the interests of the people. In their propaganda the Salvadoran and U.S. governments nevertheless still try to present the goal of the FMLN as a "totalitarian regime."

The reader of this book by Nidia Díaz must never lose sight of the reality of El Salvador today. They must understand that her testimony is just one example of what has happened in the struggle of thousands of Salvadorans and reflects the courage and dedication which continue to guide and inspire Salvadoran revolutionaries in their fight for real democracy in our country.

We are anxious that *I was never alone* will demonstrate to the reader the great and incorruptible strength of these Salvadoran revolutionaries, of whom Nidia Díaz is a typical example.

Francisco Jovel (Roberto Roca)
Member of the FMLN General Command

Somewhere in El Salvador
February 1990

These are words that have flowed through the inspiration of the men and women who day by day struggle for liberty. It is they who are crafting the best possible legacy for humankind and it is they who have led me by the hand.

In the sharing of my experiences I have simply tried to weave the garment of history from the feelings and ideas that it provided me, writing about the daily experiences born of the humble love and pain that we share.

In the name of my people I want to express our gratitude to all of you who in one form or another made it possible for this testimony to come to light.

Nidia
July 30, 1987

Part One

Wounded, captured in combat by a Yankee

• Chapter 1 •

Having neither a saint's revelation nor the clairvoyance of a seer; neither the imagination of a magician nor the premonition of a witch, I could not have foreseen what was to happen on that day. April 18, 1985, seemed normal, ordinary, like any other day. A day of challenges, of courage, of testing our convictions; of steadfastly confronting a reality that thousands would like to know and share with the children of Farabundo[1] – a reality of love, creativity and revolution. But for me that day brought with it the surprise of dying, of surviving, and then being born again. How did it come about?

"The lights! Careful, they'll detect us! We have to strictly follow procedure."

"Our defense should be circular...The ambush must be bold..."

This is how it was the night before as we looked at the maps, and discussed the plans. The FMLN guerrilla movement was preparing a major shift, a deepening in the people's war. The government was preparing itself to avoid defeat.

As we celebrated the birthdays of Miguel and Milton, apprehension hung heavily in the air. At about one in the afternoon the 0-2 aircraft, the "Push and Pull," appeared over Angostura,[2] like a bad omen of things to come. The thunder of a rocket announced the approach of the dark helicopter clouds and their rain of bullets.

"The backpacks!"

"Choppers!"

Ahead were two scout helicopters; ten more approached from the southeast. The security squadron formed a ringed defense;

---

1. The Farabundo Martí National Liberation Front (FMLN) takes its name from the 1930s revolutionary leader Farabundo Martí.

2. La Angostura is a settlement in the village of Cerros de San Pedro, in San Esteban Catarina of the Department of San Vicente in El Salvador.

the high ground was taken by the *compas*,[1] but at that moment we did not have any machine guns on the hill. The battle began.

I had made serious mistakes. Cupertino, my personal security guard, was running an errand. José, the radio operations man, was in another hut about 400 meters away. About twenty minutes before, I had sent the head of the unit to do some scouting.

I threw the backpack on my back and moved with the communications crew to a better position. The whole of the terrain was totally disadvantageous and barren. To set out for El Guayabal we had to get to the lowest part of the valley which meant crossing an open slope. We divided into two groups. There was no time for camouflage.

Which way: right or left? And from the stream to the hillside, which way from there? We could hear the hammering of machine guns about 150 meters away. The whirring of the helicopter approached. Such is the time of decisions, the moments, the instants. I kept thinking that infantry troops would arrive and that we did not have favorable tactical conditions for a skirmish. I started down the gradient on a stretch about 300 meters long, hurrying to get to the bottom in order to join the other *compas* and from there take up a better position. I thought that I could do it quickly. Two of them were about seventy-five meters away from me as we had not wanted to move in concentration. We were going down in column formation. I was slowed down by my cumbersome right foot: I had had two pins implanted when I broke it on January 22, 1980, at a mass demonstration by the popular organizations.

Suddenly, although we should have foreseen it, there were two helicopters ahead of us, a Huey UH-IH and a Hughes 500 reconnoitering for a troop landing.

"Down!" I ordered.

They sighted the *compas* and another woman *compa*, all without camouflage, who were about thirty meters behind me. I wore an olive green uniform. The ground was totally barren. I wanted to be a rock, to simply turn into a leaf or a clump of grass. Anything to be hidden. The bursts from the machine-gun started;

---

1. *Compas* is short for *compañero* (comrade; also companion, friend).

a rain of fire came out of the sky, a rain not from the mythological gods but of human origin.

A cold sweat swept over my body. I felt the beating of my heart making my chest explode to the sound of the bullets which razed me and jumped around as if trying to find a hit. I felt found out, cornered. I thought a thousand things in a fraction of a second. Maybe this was the end. But this way? In this manner? Like a worm! And one crushed by a dwarf at that! No, not like this...! I violently resented that this could be. I had survived so many years of struggle, of clandestine work in the cities, of peasant organizing, of the guerrilla struggle, and the last six encounters of this year. My mind raced. I only had to decide: to die crushed or to die discharging flashes of victory, of love and hate accumulated throughout the centuries. This is it, Nidia! I told myself. It's now or never! I squeezed hard the trigger of my rifle. One, two bursts.

I was riddled with bullets. I hadn't fired the second shot when my arm was immobilized. My rifle fell and my left foot would not move. Two wounds! Damn! I'd screwed up! And now? The wait. What to do? The helicopters left, but the "cart"[1] was still above me. How many rockets were falling around me? They seemed to be endless. I was waiting for one to fall on me. One of them killed Juanita, the radio operator. I would find out much later that she was completely charred. They had set the hillside on fire. The sun was blistering. It was burning me, suffocating me. Shrapnel was falling on my legs. I could hear the fighting about 300 meters away.

The *compas* did not even imagine the situation I was in. I hoped that they, at least, could get out of there.

• Chapter 2 •

The helicopters flew over the hillside again. They came over me, shooting in bursts. This time they were trying to finish me

---

1. Cart or *carreta* is a popular term used to describe the "Push and Pull" plane in the war zone

18

off. The "Push and Pull" gained altitude and was gone. Many bullets had gone through my backpack. One of those reached my back; another traveled through my left leg. Despite the pain, I started to reflect on my life. I had lived through the joy of struggling for my people and had left a seed: my fourteen years of guerrilla struggle would be the only inheritance I was leaving my son, my little big man. I yearned for the nightmare to end, for my blood to empty out and break my will to live.

They were still firing when the A-37 appeared. It seemed that even the daylight itself was shattered into a thousand pieces, just like it must have seemed in Vietnam. Three bombs fell about 100 meters from me. And the one for me? It fell about thirty meters away but did not go off.[1] What luck! A heat wave pushed me down, precisely at the moment I searched for my rifle. I had left it behind me.

The two helicopters were there again, not shooting, just reconnoitering, exploring. The short grass was burning, it reached my right hand and my hair. I could not stand the pain! I pretended to be dead. The Hughes 500 came down to five meters above the ground. It was on top of me, maneuvering, leaning in towards me. I thought they were going to fire a shot of mercy at me. They observed me; I was the target. Something had caught their attention. I later learnt that they thought I was Nicaraguan or Cuban because of my features.

I no longer responded to pain. I began to lose consciousness. Everything swirled. I felt nothing.

Someone took a risk. In the midst of battle he got off the chopper, squatted down and put out the flames on my body. He snatched me up as the evidence which he had not been able to produce before. He thought he had scored a winner.

Between consciousness and unconsciousness I felt the soldiers searching my body. At first I thought it was a *compa*, but when I heard the helicopter I understood the terrible reality. I opened my eyes. That yellow glove! Before I could reach my knife, he twisted my hand.

He was blond, bearded, athletic, with "Ray Ban" Polaroid

---

1. The *compañeros* later de-activated this bomb and used its explosive material.

sunglasses. A Yankee![1] He looked at me through his glasses with an expression of triumph. He put the barrel of his gun to my temple. Everything was spinning, the noise was unbearable. I knew I was in their power. I passed out.

When I came to again, tears were streaming down my cheeks. I was airborne. I noticed that the co-pilot was maneuvering in the air once more. They wanted to throw me out but the pilot refused.

My tears came from anger, not pain; I did not even whimper. I looked at the backpack with all my work documents. To think that I had put together a synthesis of all my life's work, that I had so carefully and so conscientiously kept those papers only for them now to be in the hands of the regime. I had planned everything to keep them safe now that winter was coming – not to hand them over to Mr. Reagan or to Duarte. Such a bitter twist of fate!

The Yankee turned my left arm even more and the pain it caused forced me to react. I felt alive but impotent. I wished I was somewhere else, able to disappear. I couldn't accept the fact that I had been captured, especially by a Yankee.

Here was the symbol of Reagan's policy. This was one of the 300 U.S. advisers in El Salvador. Here, in front of me, stood one of the enemies of humanity – a symbol of the false sovereignty of those who sell their country. Since the intervention against Sandino in Nicaragua, the U.S. hold over Central America had spread. They had effortlessly invaded Honduras and from there moved against the Nicaraguans and ourselves.

What shame! In a military sense, I had been beaten in this battle. They now had me physically, and they had my papers. I did not want to see what was going to happen and so I tried to jump out of the chopper into the void. There was a struggle and I once again lost consciousness.

---

1. A *Newsweek* article of November 3, 1986 pointed out that according to General Blandon, the North American was Wally Grasheim, a mercenary. Towards the end of 1985, in a private interview, the Cuban-American mercenary Félix Rodríguez (alias Max Gómez) asserted that he had participated in the capture of Commander Nidia Díaz. He repeated this in 1986 when he appeared as a witness in the Irangate-Contra case and in other conversations with journalists. In his book *Shadow Warrior: The CIA Hero of a Hundred Unknown Battles*, Rodríguez boasted of his his role in the capture.

• Chapter 3 •

So there I was – the gringo with his gun aimed at my throat. How could this be possible? I should have died; it was the moment for me to die, I thought. The centuries of struggle and victory, the faces and the bloodshed of my people passed before my eyes. I imagined caressing the olive skin of my son...I stopped thinking.

I renewed my struggle to force both the gringo and myself out of the chopper. I fainted again...His face was always before me. The incessant noise. I was their trophy.

We landed at the Air Force Base. I'd been there before. My first thoughts were what if somebody recognized me and took revenge on my brother-in-law, or hurt my family! I was in great anguish, imagining everything that could happen! And what now? They were carrying me off the chopper. I could feel myself fading, my body loosening up, consciousness leaving me.

I came to on a stretcher, smelling the stench of my own blood and sweat. I could hear the purring of the vehicle. I didn't want to die. What awaited me now? The usual fate of the disappeared, like Luis Díaz, Tony Handal,[1] Saul Villalta,[2] Janeth Samour[3]? Was this to be my fate, too? Was it now my turn?

I told myself that I shouldn't be afraid to die at their hands; thousands of men and women before me had not been afraid, nor the thousands who will come after me. It is through our deaths that the history of our people will be played out.

Nidia, I told myself, you mustn't faint again! You are in their power: don't try to take your life again. You must make an effort to overcome. Now is the moment to fill yourself with courage and

---

1. Tony Handal, President of the Architectural Association. He was captured and disappeared on November 11, 1980, by members of the Armed Forces of El Salvador.

2. Saul Villalta, leader of the National Resistance (RN), disappeared in August 1982.

3. Janeth Samour was captured by the National Guard on December 30, 1984, along with Maximina Reyes. She was tortured and disappeared.

21

prepare to wage the greatest struggle of your life. This is a serious situation but you must win. You can't give up yet!

Once in the infirmary, they violently tore off my shirt. I paid no attention, I was watching their expressions. I was taken to a room filled with peering eyes. "I am a prisoner of war!" I said. "I fall under the protection of the Geneva accords. I want to meet with the International Red Cross. Why do you ask who I am? You know who I am! I am a prisoner of war, wounded in combat. I demand that the accords are implemented. No! I don't want an I.V.! I want to die!"

"So, who are you?" they kept repeating.

"What's it to you? Ask the Yankee! Why was it a Yankee who captured me and not one of you? Aren't you ashamed?"

"This is a big fish," one of them announced over the walkie-talkie to his superior.

"Where is your self respect? It was a Yankee and not a Salvadoran!"

"Your rifle, was it an M-16? One of the ones you got from the Vietnamese?"

My rifle had not been taken; all they had was the ammunition I carried in my harness.

"No, it was one of the ones we took from you at El Paraíso,[1] in the same way we have captured all our rifles, those same weapons which continually cause you casualties."

The doctor arrived. He looked at me only from a distance. "Give her an I.V., wash her hair, and change her clothes," he ordered peremptorily, before he turned and left.

The Yankee who had captured me came in. He picked up my pants which were patched on the seat, the same pants I had worn to the peace negotiations with the government at La Palma in October 1984. He laughed and showed them to the other advisers and officers present. Next, he looked at my badly worn boots. They had my watch, my earrings, everything. Even the "doe seeds" given to me by Commander Susana who had received them from a grandmother in Chalatenango as a good luck charm.

They divided my belongings among themselves. The Yankee approached me. "Hi!" he said smiling.

---

1. El Paraíso was the site of a guerrilla attack on an army barracks on December 30, 1983.

"Son of a bitch Yankee!" I yelled. I tried to spit at him, but I only splattered myself. He patted me on the shoulder and left.

"Why don't you just shut up!" somebody shouted at me.

One of them came in with the I.D. I carried in my pants and my son's photo. "Are you María Marta Valladares?"

"What do you think?"

"Is this your legal name? What is your *nom de guerre*?"

"You figure it out."

"What were you doing in that area? Is that where your camp was? Who is your commander? Answer me! Are you deaf?"

"Who are you?" another officer repeated.

I had assumed they knew who I was, that they had targeted me, that they knew who and what was there in Angostura that day.

They brought in Osmín, a nine-year old boy. I recognized him. He was the son of one of the *compañeros* of the Angostura settlement. He had been wounded and captured.

"Do you know her?"

"No, I don't know her."

"And you him?"

"No, I don't know him."

Almost all of them left. A remaining officer commented, "So, babe, why have you gotten yourself involved in all of this? Why? Look at yourself! Why don't you get out of it? Start your life again."

"The life of a guerrilla's no good for you," said another.

A sergeant approached me; I thought he might know me from someplace else. He asked me if I wanted a sandwich and Coke and handed them to me. Tears welled up in his eyes. I was surprised. I had not expected to encounter such a gesture in the midst of my enemy. But of course! I remembered him from my brother-in-law's house: they used to play chess together. I drank some of the Coke.

I was moved to another room. Two soldiers were left to guard me. An officer entered. "I know you," he began. "Don't you remember? We were in preparatory together at the university. Why are you involved in *this*?"

"And you, why are you involved in this?" I asked.

"I like the military career and can get a lot out of it. But, you?"

"Our people have been forced to take up arms. We love peace, we love life. This is an unjust war that has been imposed on us."

"We too, are fighting for peace."

"Sure, the peace of the graveyard, of hunger, of injustice."

"You're wrong. We don't want totalitarianism, or to be invaded by the Russians."

"Do I look Russian to you?"

"They hide the truth from you. They lie to you."

After about thirty minutes I did not want to go on talking. I could not stand the pain. They had not even given me an aspirin. He continued talking, but his voice became more and more distant.

• Chapter 4 •

"Look," he was saying, "we are fighting in order to end all this. But you guerrillas refuse to lay down your arms. You have been defeated in combat, there is no way you can win against us. We are more numerous, we have more resources, we have more fire power."

Without hesitating, I replied: "And you are more afraid! You know that your cause is not just, that you simply defend the interests of the empire. You have soiled yourselves in the filth and have sucked the blood of the best children of our nation."

"The people support us, and other governments recognize El Salvador as a democratic country," he argued.

"You know that's a lie! Duarte, our so-called president, is nothing more than a puppet of the United States – like the rest of you. And besides, you live in fantasy land if you believe in a military victory over the FMLN."

"Can't you see that things have changed, that we have carried out reforms?"

"That's a lie! The famous reforms of 1979 and the democracy that you talk so much about have all been drowned in blood."

Neither of us could stop; it was a confrontation between two people who had once shared something in common but who had ultimately opted for two very different roads in life, and were now poles apart.

"You are all just hot air," he continued. "You think that words alone can make things happen. You think that you're so smart. Do you think your taking power will make the slightest difference? Wake up to yourself – taking power is not so easy..."

"We know that. But you can't fool anyone. Real life shows that..."

"Forget it! You're finished, but I'm opening a door for you, a way out. You are defeated. Look at yourself: you're all cut to pieces, burned all over. You're pathetic. Just wait and see."

Suddenly the argument stopped, and instead he began to interrogate me. "What is your *nom de guerre*? What do they call you? Are you Marta? You have a beautiful child, who's his father? The man in the picture? Is that him?"

"I don't know. I don't know anything. I don't feel like answering."

"You have a son, don't you?"

"Yes, I have a very beautiful child. I love him very much," I said.

"I don't believe it – you're without love! That area where you were captured, was that your camp?"

At that point he was interrupted by two officers hurriedly entering the room, holding some photographs in their hands. "So, you're Nidia Díaz, eh?" one of them said looking me straight in the eye. "Well, well, *the* Nidia Díaz?"

Silence. Everyone looked at me. They went out and left me with two soldiers. How did they find out? Easy...they had searched through my backpack and found papers, letters, notebooks, cassettes, all addressed to Nidia. That led them to the conclusion that it must be me. This was confirmed by photos from the negotiations at La Palma. So, they had not attacked that day with the intention of capturing me!

There was no doubt now that the power struggle between us would intensify. I knew that they would certainly try to take advantage of my weak physical condition. They were debating what to do with me, how to take advantage of my capture. It did not take them long. Two of them came in, dressed in civilian clothes. "What's your name?" they began.

"You already know my name."

"Where does your family live?"

"I don't know. Is that your plan, to seek out my family? It's been years since I've seen them, I don't know where they live."

"Was that your camp where you were captured? Who else was there? What other commanders were there? What were you doing?"

"I was hiking, picking mangos."

They looked at each other in anger and left. Shortly afterwards one soldier returned and told me to rest because I was in a bad way. But I could not rest; I was tense and remained on the alert. Time passed; it was dawn. If I closed my eyes, they talked to me. They had no intention of letting me sleep.

Hours passed. I found it difficult to calculate time. They transferred me to another room and to a different stretcher. The room was huge, without any furniture. Soldiers, officers, and interrogators dressed in civilian clothes all came and went. More time passed. The I.V. dried up.

A short, light-skinned officer came in. He was dressed in camouflage fatigues. He brought a tape recorder. Slowly, he inserted a cassette. A woman's voice began to play: " ...on February 5 we buried Arturo Ramos in the Gardens of Remembrance. For a long time – several days – our dear *compañero* struggled between life and death. He was in a clandestine hospital. His sister, who knows about nursing, provided all his care. Leticia, Mario, and myself went to his funeral..." He then turned it off.

He continued watching me and said, "Right now all our intelligence units are working on resolving this case. We're going to destroy the whole citywide network of the PRTC.[1] And you're going to help a lot. Did you hear me? This cassette was in your backpack. You were also carrying a lot of papers."

"I did not have that cassette!"

"Yes you did, and a lot of other things. Yes, even some things in code."

"Well if you're so intelligent, interpret them yourselves."

He played the tape again and began to ask trivial questions. I did not answer him. I could only think of what might happen to the *compañeros* in the city and how it would be my fault. I started

1. The PRTC is the Central American Revolutionary Workers Party of which Nidia Díaz is a leader.

to imagine the possibilities and the ways in which they could resolve the situation. I was despairing. All I could do was to trust in the conspiratorial capacity of my *compas*.

"Collaborate, Nidia! What's your real name? Where does your family live? Where is your camp? What were you doing in that place?"

This continuous and monotonous repetition of the same questions and my own thoughts about the *compañeros* were interrupted by the entrance of "Horse" Perdomo, Captain Perdomo, commander of the Long-Range Reconnaissance Patrols (PRAL). "Get out!" he told the other interrogator. "I'll do the talking." The officer left. "Look at you; you're pathetic," he spat. He stood sideways, very arrogantly, with a superior air. "You no longer remember me, that's good. I'm very proud of my boys. They did great work."

"But they still have a lot to learn from the guerrillas."

"Oh, yeah? No kidding! Do you realize that there were only ten men involved in that operation? Who did this to you?" He pointed to my arm.

"Ten men?" I asked, confused.

"Yes, ten seasoned men."

"Ten of your men?"

"Of course, one of the PRAL units."

"So how come I was captured by a Yankee?"

According to President Reagan, Central America had become, in those last few years, the most important challenge for the United States since Vietnam. And it was in our little country, our little Tom Thumb, that they had engaged in the largest counter-insurgency war in recent times.

"Do you think that we are going to stand by with our arms folded while you're helped by the Russians? You have bases in Nicaragua, you travel to Cuba all the time," he continued.

"I've never been to Cuba."

"Well then, you're a fool! The other leaders go around living the high life while here you are, so pitiful. I am proud of my boys. You know, Nidia, you guys make so many mistakes. The night before last, we detected some lights in the area where we captured you. So yesterday morning my boys went reconnoitering and we sent the air support. They are well trained and pretty effective aren't they?"

What he said confirmed my suspicions about the night of the birthday celebration for Milton and Miguel. It also confirmed what we knew about American aid. Even though the Kissinger Report rejected the direct use of U.S. troops and advisers, the reality of the war had forced the participation of those advisers in combat. And this would inevitably continue and progressively increase, in spite of their differences with the Salvadoran officers. Meanwhile, the FMLN continued to advance because of the weakness of the puppet army. The enormous amount of aid that they received only helped delay their ultimate defeat.

The interrogators never let up: "Nidia, collaborate! Where is Mario? We're going to find him anyway. We're going to destroy the urban guerrillas, the *Mardoqueo Cruz* Commandos. This cassette was in your bag and it's going to be very useful. Pay attention! What can you tell us about Leticia? And Roberto?"

On and on all day until dusk, question after question, until they took me away on the stretcher.

• Chapter 5 •

I was in the van again, blindfolded, lying face down on the floor. I had not eaten or slept, my nerves were shattered. I had never felt such anguish. Because I knew the city so well, I could tell what direction we were taking out of the Air Force Base.

They put a sheet over my head. I did not believe they were going to kill me, at least not for the moment. Did they see my capture as a political victory? Would I end up like Janeth? Were they planning something different for me?

We went down Venezuela Boulevard, perhaps towards Police Headquarters or the office of the military chiefs of staff. The van was stuffy, I couldn't breathe. I could feel them watching me. Nidia, stay alert! I reminded myself. My mind was a blank. I only knew that I had a mission to fulfil and that I had to continue struggling.

We arrived at the National Police Headquarters. There were unfamiliar footsteps. They removed the sheet. I could see curious eyes peering through the windows. After a while, a doctor came in to check me over. In spite of my condition he did nothing. My right hand was twisted and paralyzed; the bullet that had penetrated my arm had destroyed the radial nerve. I needed a cast for my left foot which was broken.

Hours passed. It was dark and the van started moving again. They took me to the Salvadoran Polyclinic where a nun X-rayed me as detectives hovered around. I was then moved back to the National Police Headquarters, to Cell 20, and spent the entire night under interrogation. In spite of my weakened state, I let not even a whimper betray my agonizing pain.

Trumpets sounded reveille. From the noises I realized it was morning. There was no way to tell from within that cell as there was no natural light and the hall lights were always on.

They took me out on a mattress, my face covered with a towel. I was inside the van again. We went to a small civilian hospital in the Flor Blanca neighborhood where I was admitted under the name of Rosa María Vásquez. An I.V. was connected; I received some basic first aid. The doctors were moved by the extent of my injuries; I could tell by their expressions as they examined the open flesh wounds on my arm.[1] They were annoyed by the continual interference by the large number of detectives sent to guard me.

"She needs at least eight days hospitalization," stated one of

---

1. On May 4, Dr. Goosby, assistant professor of the School of Medicine at the University of San Francisco, and Dr. Stuart Kimble from Berkeley examined Nidia and provided separate diagnoses. Dr. Goosby's diagnosis included the following:

Díaz is a young, 32-year old woman. She was wounded two weeks ago in the right forearm, the right shoulder and the left foot. Even now she complains of her inability to use her right hand and of pain in her left foot, which occasionally drains purulent matter. The patient does not report having had a temperature or chills, but has had twitching of the first and second fingers of the right forearm. She also reports pain in her chest when taking deep breaths, without having a cold or congestion.

Extremities: right scapula bullet wound...the right arm has second-degree burns from the elbow running down the forearm; right forearm has one entry and one exit bullet wounds; the left thigh has a bullet wound, entry on the side of the thigh and exit below the knee; six superficial abrasions on the same thigh; one on the right. *Right hand*: cannot move the wrist completely; the thumb cannot be extended nor retracted; loss of feeling. *Left foot*: side entry and exit bullet wound; does not appear to be draining.

It was not possible to obtain an X-ray examination nor any of the medical records from those who have been charged with her care. Discussion of the case was not possible.

the doctors.

An officer went outside with a walkie-talkie in his hand. The doctors seemed shocked when, striding back into the room, he announced: "Well, she won't even get eight hours!"

I thought the trip would never end; my agony increased with each passing moment. Once I was back in Cell 20, a military nurse opened an I.V. valve. I began to sweat, I was freezing. The interrogators noticed that I was fainting. They became alarmed and removed the I.V. "Don't be stupid! Can't you see we want her alive!"

Many hours later, there were still six interrogators holding vigil over me as if I were dead. "So, was that your camp, Nidia?" they started again.

"No."

"How many were there with you?"

"It was a small unit. They died fighting. I am a prisoner of war! I want to see the International Red Cross."

"Don't be a fool! Your comrades abandoned you, they left you wounded. You were only a burden. Can't you understand? It's the truth. We intercepted their communications and that was their plan. We were signaled by the informer who infiltrated your ranks when the right time came to pick you up."

"That's a lie! And even if it were true, it makes no difference to me!"

"What are the plans of the FMLN?"

"To build a just society."

"We're asking you what their plans are for the next few days."

"We're going to defeat you; we're going to defeat all your tactics. One by one, until you have nothg left."

"You are the ones who are defeated. Don't you understand?"

• Chapter 6 •

A long time passed; I had overcome my sleepiness. I could not close my eyes. They were waiting for me to get tired, for me to complain. In fact, I was almost at that point. Luis, Janeth, how did you do it? Is this it? I asked myself. After the battle, comes a war of words? Not so simple. All the reasons why I struggled were also at stake in this new war.

"How are you feeling?"

"How do you want me to feel? I'm fine!"

"We want to let someone know about you. Where does your family live?"

"Go to the war zones – that's where my family lives."

"What about Camilo?"

Perhaps it was afternoon when several men came in. One was nicknamed "Shorty." He was very tall and obviously a killer. He blindfolded me and lifted me up. They opened an iron door to Cell 21, where they conducted interrogations. "Well, Nidia, we're now going to begin working the way we should," he said firmly.

Silence. No one spoke. I was seated, still blindfolded. From under the blindfold I could count about nine pairs of shoes. They were standing around me in a semicircle.

What to do? The struggle was about to start again. A chance to test myself: a real trial by fire which may be the biggest challenge I'd ever have to face. I reviewed my situation: OK, what are their advantages over me? None, Nidia, none! They have not won. Besides you have your people, your struggle is just, and you represent higher principles. History's on your side.

I took the initiative and shouted aggressively: "Well, gentlemen, what are you waiting for? Here's my arm, or if you want, here's the other." I stretched out my burned right arm toward them. "And here's my tongue. You can start. I'm not going to tell you anything!"

"You're wrong. Don't worry, nothing's going to happen to you, we're not going to torture you," they said.

"I know where we are. I know who you are! You're the death squad murderers, disguised as the law. You are the "Children of Cain."[1] You're going to interrogate me, you're about to torture me. I know this cubicle, and those others..."

"No! That's all your imagination."

"Hundreds of my *compañeros* have come through here, our countrymen, whom you have tortured and assassinated while

---

1. Children of Cain is the name that the intelligence unit of the National Police gave itself, headed by an officer who bears that name. They were responsible for the cruellest and most bestial tortures suffered by those who were detained.

trying to drag information out of them. I can feel their blood, their warmth here to comfort me..."

"Shut up! Nothing's going to happen to you. Just understand that you must cooperate with us. We're democratic, peaceful people."

"Lies!"

"It'll go better if you're quiet and don't talk so much shit."

"First I'll die! You hear me! I'll die!"

I wasn't hysterical, though I probably should have been, given the circumstances. How many years I had spent steeling myself for this! To die by their hands, to be tortured, disappeared. I had worked in the urban front and had lived clandestinely in their midst, conspiring to resist and win, to do my duty, to die honorably. And then, suddenly, there I was! I knew my moral strength. I was convinced that I could not be broken. I could ignore the wounds and the burns, and other forms of torture. What I had to watch was my spirit. I had to pay attention to everything they said, to gauge the moment. Maybe they had already decided not to kill me. Even if they hadn't, I had to tell them what I thought of them. I did not have to hide who I was. They obviously knew. We were face to face, without any subterfuge. I had to counter what had been a military gain on their part.

Then something totally unexpected occurred. One of them, or perhaps he was someone allowed in although not one of the interrogators, violently pulled off my blindfold. "Look at me, look at me, never forget me. You guys are going to win! You're going to win! Remember me," he pleaded.

I was quite bewildered: How could this be? What were they trying to do? Whatever the reasons for his actions, his words came as a timely acknowledgement for me. I put the blindfold on again. After so much time wearing it the light bothered me. For a long time, things appeared to be still. It seemed as if they had all left. I could not support myself well in the chair.

The next morning I was carried to Cell 20. The blindfold was removed and a hooded man entered. He started taking my picture, from the front and sideways. So, they were going to register me! They blindfolded me and took me back to Cell 21 where the interrogation began once more: "Where are the rest of the papers? Where, where, where is Roberto? And the other camps? Where do you carry out work? Where, where, what place do you go to meet? Where? What place?" They kept it up for hours.

Nightfall. The trumpet sounded. Where, I thought, are all those disappeared? Where is my son, Alejandrito? What is my little big man doing right now? He would be four years old on June 2. Had they tried to kill him? Were they holding him here? Poor little one, to have been born and raised in time of war! I wondered what he was feeling. And what if they tortured him in front of me? I shuddered. I couldn't bear to think of anything so monstrous.

"Are you asleep? Wake up! We're here to work, not to sleep."

"You're working, not me."

My thoughts transported me to the hills and valleys of my Cuscatlán, to the peak of Guazapa, in the FMLN-held region. All those times we had traveled through it in single column to reach the command post!...El Salitre, El Roblar...long walks at night, sometimes five hours in total darkness. The army could have detected us from its military posts at El Roblar and El Caballito, from up high. They had been gruelling walks, relieved only by the stops we could make when we came to a river. The wintry cold water of Las Pacayas. All the fruits of El Salitre. How many we ate before setting out: mangos, guavas, oranges, sapodillas...ah! how I loved sapodillas. Along the way we would have the chance to eat olives, nances, jocotes, oranges, and sometimes sugar cane.

We would climb up and down the hillsides, one meadow after another. I always believed it was the loud frogs croaking that helped keep me awake. We walked alert and in silence. Whenever I had the chance I would pick flowers to carry on my pack. I could still smell their fragrance: white and purple bell-flowers with their white stems. Nights filled with fireflies. It was the smell of the flowers that warned us of our proximity to one of the settlements in the area: Palo Grande, El Roble, Llano Rancho...all desolate ruins now. Yet the *compas* are still there.

Heroic Land
(Hills of San Pedro, June 14, 1985)

Ten years on,
your earth
your soil
which watched me grow
which saw me organizing
the will of the people,
today watched
my blood run
watched my capture
and you're the only witness!

Was it bad luck?
Was it adversity?
Was it coincidence?
Or was it caused by
tactical blunders in
our revolutionary work?
The rounds of the machine-guns
razed the slope
the rockets unloaded
their explosive entrails
over your burning hillsides,
and the 500 lb. bombs
shattered the sound
of your natural beauty.
Was it a nightmare or reality?
It was reality and you were the only witness!

Heroic land,
witness of my courage or cowardice,
my heroism or martyrdom
my mistaken, imprudent or correct decision
my historic responsibility or irresponsibility.
Which was it? What happened? What am I?
It all becomes the same
at such an unfortunate moment.

There is no question, that day
all the factors came together.
Everything was ready
for a surprise response. For a test, a trial run!
We violated everything: the plan, the norms, the rules.
All in order to receive Mr. Reagan's gift.

Heroic land,
a Yankee tramples on your soul,
he kills you and with his claws
he captures the bird bloodied with life.
The steel monster
took flight with the bird
which was close to death but survived.
That bird now lives and will return to be free
to organize the people.
And you
heroic land
will be its witness!

Part Two

Inhuman interrogation ...never yielding

• Chapter 7 •

The interrogation continued. And to think, I told myself, that you now find yourself here, face to face with these immoral soldiers, part of a fratricidal army. Our people, the people of El Salvador, must pay the cost of this war many times over with their lives, while Reagan supplies the weapons.

"Let's see Nidia, how many years have we set back the revolution because of all the documents that fell into our hands when we captured you?" said one of the interrogators trying to pierce me with guilt.

"That's what you'd like to think," I responded. "But the FMLN is better prepared than that: by this time, all the operations that might have been placed at risk will have been changed."

"No, honey, you're not as smart as you think," he scoffed.

"Do you think that we can't foresee the possible capture of one of our leaders? Many people are aware of my capture, and they know I was carrying papers."

"You shouldn't trust so much in the FMLN. They are going to blame you for everything we have been doing to them. We are taking their camps, their leaders. Thanks to the information you provided us, we are searching them out and finishing them off," he added ironically.

"Even if, as you say, you're able to beat back many of them, there will always be at least one person left who will carry on our struggle."

"You'll never get out of here. You'll rot in here, baby. How many people do you have? Let's see, how many people are in your party, the PRTC? Speak up! What, aren't you listening? Are you going to say that you don't know that either?"

"On principle..."

"Principle? You guys have no principles; you don't even believe in God, you're communists, assassins!"

"And you?" I replied angrily. "You, in the name of God, torture and assassinate our people; and for your God, impose a reign of terror and death. And you dare to talk to me of God!"

"We've never killed anybody!"

"Oh, no? You have sent thousands of humble, defenseless Salvadorans to their eternal rest. When you detain the peasants, dragging them out of their homes, they're so scared they even forget their own names."

"Go on, go on," another laughed scornfully.

"And, as if that weren't bad enough, in addition to asking them for their I.D. card and their travel documents, you demand that they show the 'Magnifica'. And if they're not carrying it, then you consider them atheists, communists who only deserve a bullet through the head."

"See, that's what I mean. You're all alike – all hot air. You all think you are so enlightened, the saviors of humanity, little angels. But do you know what you really are?" he laughed.

"Neither angels nor fools."

"You're insolent, that's what you are! What does 'sweet orange' mean?"

"I don't know."

"What is 'the edge'? Where do you get your weapons from?"

"From the United States. First, Reagan sends them to you, then..."

"We use them to capture you, just like we've done with you," one of them interrupted.

"No, first Reagan sends the weapons to you; then you use them in your genocide against the people. Then we snatch them away from you. It's a vicious cycle which shouldn't continue."

"Ah, yes! So how will it end?"

"By Salvadorans resolving our conflicts among ourselves."

"First you guerrillas will have to lay down your arms."

"So, you're afraid! Why can't we reach a political settlement through dialogue? Couldn't we together provide a comprehensive solution to the national crisis?"

"You're crazy!"

"Is your president crazy? He says *he's* for dialogue. Is the government crazy? How about the minister for defense, Vides Casanova?" I commented sarcastically.

"Well, they can talk whatever shit they want; but in this country no one is going to negotiate with terrorists."

"You can't talk with this one, that's for sure," said another of the interrogators.

I think it was morning. I had already spent seven days without sleep. I had become almost used to the sick feeling in the pit of my stomach, it no longer seemed strange. I was slipping out of my chair. The bullet in my back was hurting me badly; the burn was raw, open skin. They would put ointment on it and then cover it up with bandages. My arm and my foot were swollen and felt like over-inflated tires.

"What's the matter? Are you in pain?" one of them asked in a jeering voice.

"No, nothing that's unusual for someone in my condition."

At last, silence. But they remained standing there; I could feel their breathing. How many were there? Perhaps six or eight men.

"I want to pee," I announced.

"Take her."

So, as they had done before, they lifted me in their arms and then into a chair, as if in a carriage. I could not hang on because of the fractures. Then they took me back to the interrogation chair.

"Baby, you should collaborate. You're finished anyway. Can't you see that's there's no other way out? No one else cares about you; no one but us."

There was another heavy silence. I put my hand on my forehead and began to sing in a slow, steady voice:

> Let nothing demoralize me,
> let nothing exasperate me,
> a guerrilla fighter's like a bull
> in the midst of a raging storm.
> They wounded me,
> they killed me,
> they captured me
> and even gave me death.
> But they never broke me...

"Sing it again, sing it. You can't stand it any more, you can't resist any more," they mocked.

"Bring me a sleeping pad!" They threw me on the mattress and squatting beside me continued firing questions; but I didn't answer. It reminded me of the stories we were told as children about limbo, or about the inferno in the Divine Comedy. I could picture the faces of those men on the other side of my blindfold. I didn't need to look at them.

"Eat!"

"I don't want to." I pushed the food away. It smelt terrible.

"It's not healthy for you to be on a hunger strike. You're weak. You're only hurting yourself. We've heard that the FMLN is going to execute you. They no longer trust you. We're the only ones who can help you now," one of them crooned in my ear.

"That's a lie! And even if it were true, I grant the FMLN the right to make a mistake."

"You'd better believe it. From now on, we're your family – your mother, your father, your husband, your son. We're your world now, can't you see? You have no other way out. If you don't collaborate with us, you will rot here. But we can help you," he insisted.

"OK, so I rot here or in El Playón,[1] or in the River Lempa, or on whatever road you're going to dump me. Things will go on with or without Nidia, that much is sure."

"So, who will take your place? Thanks to you and your papers we're capturing everyone." They were desperate to plant the seed of guilt in me; to have me weaken and begin to trust them.

"And if you were to turn up dead, wrapped in the flag of the FMLN? You don't believe people would think that the FMLN was responsible? After all, it wouldn't be the first time that you resorted to killing each other."

"You think you can go on fooling people. You can do whatever you want with me; I'm not afraid of death."

Time passed. The questions kept coming, but I barely heard them. Then, suddenly they announced they were taking me out to see the press.

"No, I won't go. I won't be used in a video that you can manipulate. I'll die first!"

"Stop fucking around! You have to go, it's the press. Can't you

---

1. El Playón is an arid place on the Pacific Coast, in Usulután, where government troops frequently abandon the bodies of those they have captured.

see that it's because Radio Venceremos[1] has been saying that the press should be allowed to come and see you?"

"And you think I'll believe you? I know your game. I won't cooperate!"

"Pick her up!"

I started to struggle, but they simply lifted up the whole mattress. I was screaming. They took me to Cell 21 and threw me on another pad. There were about ten interrogators, a doctor, and some detectives. They took off my blindfold. In a fury I began to bang my head on the wall. They became alarmed and said I had gone crazy.

• Chapter 8 •

I heard footsteps. Here they come, I thought. I rolled over on my stomach to hide my face. I felt floodlights on me. I was sure they were trying to film a video. I turned to look and saw many cameras focused on me.

All the press were there. I recognized reporters who were at the negotiations at La Palma. But how were they ever allowed in? I wanted to tell them what was happening to me. But at that instant the reporters were taken away again. Damn! I had wasted ten minutes and the opportunity to denounce my captors.

Another group of reporters was brought in. I sat up and began to speak: "I am a prisoner of war. I was wounded in combat on April 18. The enemy dropped bombs on the civilian population. I was captured by a Yankee. I'm undergoing interrogation. They found papers on me, important papers, which they're going to try to use. I believe a political solution to the conflict is possible; the FMLN is struggling for that objective."

The officers quickly removed the press from the cell. They were furious. I had denounced them to their face.

Immediately afterwards, four delegates from the International Red Cross arrived, including Martin Fulher, delegation head for El Salvador, whom I had met at La Palma; Kurt Seller, International Red Cross representative at the National Police Headquar-

---

1. Radio Venceremos is an FMLN rebel radio station.

ters; Dr. Muheim; and the man in charge of dealing with the press, Roland Bigler. They greeted me cordially and asked how I was feeling. They told me that my capture and my imprisonment had been acknowledged. I kept staring at them in disbelief. A deep sense of relief ran through my body. So perhaps my fate was not to be disappeared after all!

The doctor checked me out and told me not to worry, that they couldn't do anything to me any more. After that, he told me, there was nothing to do but to wait and monitor my medical situation, for which they were going to assume responsibility.

"I can't stand the exhaustion and the pain any more," I allowed myself to moan. "I need to rest for at least a couple of hours. Don't they understand? What day is today?"

"Today is Wednesday, April 24, and it's 7 p.m. We have been asking to be allowed to see you for days but they wouldn't let us until now. The Armed Forces' press office did not announce your capture until April 22. The FMLN approached us and the Church, urging us to do something from the beginning;[1] but we could not get any information on you until the start of the week. All we can do is see you and reassure you that everything will be OK. You must rest and take it easy."

I put my left hand over my face; I felt I was about to cry. I'm not disappeared, I thought to myself. I had been preparing for that all along. To be tortured, to die by their hand just like so many others, the way that Janeth must have died, and Aguiñada too.[2] But I was not so prepared for this psychological war and these new and shameless methods of softening you up. They are so cynical, I thought. Why are they treating me like this? I remember when I read the book *Kidnapping and the Hood and Clandestine Jails*; but now more than ever I remember Benedet-

---

1. On April 19 the FMLN had reported my capture to the archbishop, the International Red Cross and to the governments of other countries so that they would intercede before President Duarte. The first public announcements were made in Radio Venceremos. On April 21 the General Command of the FMLN issued a communique warning what the High Command of the Armed Forces and Duarte might be doing to Commanders Janeth Samour, Nidia Díaz and Miguel Castellanos.

2. Mario Aguiñada, a fighter of the Armed Liberation Forces of the Communist Party, had been captured in combat on April 15, 1985, in Cerros de San Pedro in the department of San Vicente. He was later disappeared.

ti's *Pedro and the Captain*, which taught me so much.

This was so much more threatening because it was so unexpected – just the way my capture had been. I had never imagined, and never prepared myself for that possibility, to be captured in the war zone, wounded like that. I had always expected to die fighting, to be captured on the urban front, or maybe as I went to and from the mountains, or perhaps at an airport. But never in the mountains. I used to tell the *compas* that if I was wounded and they couldn't evacuate me, that they should allow me to die. It had never once occurred to me that it could be this way. And now? It was all so violent – the capture and the interrogation. It all seemed so strange, and yet I should have realized this could happen, from the first time I heard of the death or disappearance of some *compa*.

"Can't you demand that they apply the Geneva Accords, the additional protocols, International Human Rights Law?" I asked them.

"Of course, Nidia. That's why we're here. But there are time stipulations and they're not willing to give an inch more. You have to go through another nine days. You must spend fifteen days in interrogation."

"In interrogation, you mean, without sleep."

"Unfortunately, it's the law – Decree No.50."

"But I don't recognize that law. OK, let's not talk about that. Let me say I'm very glad to see you, that your presence alone means a lot to me, even if you can't do anything else."

"Should we let your family know?"

"No! If my mother seeks you out, let her know that I'm well. Tell the people of my country, tell the FMLN, that I'm well, of sound mind, and that they will never break me here. Tell them that I love them and that I will survive, no matter how difficult it may be."

I was shivering. I felt cold. They noticed it and looked at each other. Their faces reflected pity at the sight of human suffering. But it seemed there was little they could do.

Blindfolded again. The darkness. This time I was sitting at a desk. The pain from my burn was unbearable. Was it infected? Maybe I had just managed to ignore the pain while being so tense and concentrating on making it through interrogation.

"Are you asleep? Wake up!" they yelled, pounding on the table.
"I'm not asleep!"
"All you did was talk shit to the press, all lies."
"It wasn't me who brought them here," I said.
"And the man in this photo, is he your husband?"
"Very funny! Her husband's a sergeant," another one said.
They all laughed.
"What rank was your companion? He's the one in the picture,
right? Listen, it's so romantic: 'My love, even though we may not
be together physically and we may never see each other again, I
will not forget you. I will always carry you with me, my love, like
a beautiful memory, like the beautiful reality that we shared.'"
"How pretty, how beautiful!" they chorused, mocking me.
"Where is this man?" they asked again and again.

• Chapter 9 •

Back in my cell, sadness began to trace ghosts in my mind. I
looked about me and counted the bricks one by one, in the same
way that I now counted my days in captivity. I smoked, although
I knew I shouldn't. Out of the darkness the background noises
came from the interrogations taking place in the cell next to mine
– hardly like falling asleep to the sound of one's lover's whispers.
Sometimes I was lucky and fell asleep suddenly, sinking into
dreams which brought my child to me once again. I would sing
him to sleep every night we were together.

> Sleep, sleep, my child
> 'cause your mama's in the fields
> working
> working, yes, working, no.
> She's going to bring you...

I had the joy of having him with me for almost two years. He
was always my friend. He kept me company in my work, though
of course, he didn't understand what was going on. Sometimes, it
seemed like he did. Once I was in bed with malaria and I had to

leave for the war zone the next day. He came close and caressed me, saying, "Mama, Mama! There's a lot of dead soldiers near the Cuscatlán Bridge." He had heard it on the news and had come to tell me. Another occasion, we were stopped at a checkpoint. They took my driver's license away and he began to scream, "Don't take my mom away, don't take my mom!" He was referring to my photograph on the license.

I remembered one afternoon we spent in the park playing at riding horses. Alejandro said I was the mare and he was the colt. I laughed a lot at everything he said. Then there was the time I helped him lose his fear of the sea...If only I could stop thinking! But so many memories flashed through my mind.

> I want to sleep from exhaustion
> so that I won't think about you.
> I want to sleep deeply,
> dreaming.
> To live in a dream.

Singing soothed me, but only for an instant. I was filled with a sweet and sad nostalgia for my loved ones. Where were they? What had happened to them? It all seemed so long ago. I felt a longing and deep hurt when I remembered the man who is my child's father and whom I loved so much. Was that love just a dream? Where in our beloved Central America could he be? Was he alive? If he were dead, where was his body? I had no answer. The war that had brought us together had now physically separated us. We taught and supported each other, learnt and grew together. It took a lot of strength and consciousness not to falter along this long, separate road.

That morning when we said goodbye his eyes grew misty. His voice was so serious when he said, "Please, take care of yourself! Remember that our child and I both rely on you."

"Will we ever meet again?" I asked him, fearfully.

"How can we know? But whatever happens, I want you to be strong and brave, and to live life to the full."

He walked away slowly, not wanting to leave. That time we hadn't even been together for forty-eight hours. I closed my eyes to try to blot out the pain. I felt like something was tearing inside of me. He waved to me with his right hand through the bus window, his sad eyes looking straight at me. I could never forget that moment – his black hair, the gleam in his eye.

Each time he saw his son, little Alejandro, the baby hugged him and would rest his head on his shoulder, without saying anything. He would say to me: "He hugs me as if he believes he'll be left without either you or me."

The last time that my mother had taken the boy to see him was in February 1984, when he was in great danger. There were times when I felt the emptiness and the loss that arises when someone you love disappears or has died. There was no end to my love for him, it came from the depths of my soul. Even though I realized I may never see him again, I would always love him in the fruit of my womb, our little Alejandro.

Before we got together we had been doing political work together for a year. Although I found him pleasant company, I never imagined we would become companions and lovers. Love played around us, silently flirting with us. Then one day, pink roses and caresses uncovered the fact that we needed and loved each other. Later, when we had the chance to share a home, we tried to share everything. We divided the chores and childcare. Despite our clandestine life we had moments of great tenderness. When we had problems or conflicts we confronted them immediately so that we were able to seal the cracks that might be starting to open. We understood each other. How could I forget him? He will remain with me until my last battle.

There are many *compas* of whom I have been very fond. We revolutionaries by our very nature are filled with great affection for our people, for our *compas*. We watch each other grow and develop along our common road. But it is impossible to have that special relationship with each one, as a man and woman. There are many *compas* who remain alone. How many of us have had the privilege of loving and being loved? How many have suffered terrible loss and disillusionment? Our view of life tends to eliminate selfishness and prevent us from being fickle. Even when a relationship ends, although it hurts, it usually ends without rancor. We find we can assimilate the experience with maturity. As we focus on the broader picture, we can more easily understand why it is that a given relationship won't work out. Our common perpective strengthens our emotional ties, the camaraderie among us. Besides, we have other problems to confront.

Many thoughts went around in my head; whether they were real or imagined it was hard to tell. I remembered the times of our coming together, and then painful separations; the periods of stable relationships; the one that had been, but could no longer be; and the one that was, but could not be at the time. Family relationships among individuals in our movement are very much subject to circumstance, inextricably linked to the struggle, especially in a war situation such as exists today in our country. Homes are broken up, people separate in order to do their duty or because the enemy takes their loved ones away. For some couples, there will be joint work in the same area for a time. But despite all this we manage to have happy times with our families.

We live with the certainty that the victory will bring us together again, to allow us to establish or renew family life. Nature tends towards wanting to make each other happy in a more permanent way. Maybe for me, it can't be again with the father of my child; but perhaps it can be with some other revolutionary who shares this road.

In the dark, empty cell I felt my soul as naked before my eyes, speaking to me of my humanity, reminding me that I was a woman, a human being with all my anxieties. In my loneliness, I did not feel alone, although at times I was overcome by a longing for the touch of my loved one. It was strange that I felt so calm. I was not tormented by matters of love. I had been happy and that was enough, although it was painful no longer being together, no longer being able to warm one another with our bodies and expressions of our mutual joy. He will always be with me, always and everywhere. He flows within me as my very lifeblood.

• Chapter 10 •

More interrogation. Again, the silence. I could feel their breathing. I remembered the session of a few days ago, when they came to tell me with great triumph that I was María Marta Valladares, and all the other stuff that Mario Zetino, an ex-PRTC member whom they had captured, had told them. How did it begin...

"Do you know Mario Zetino?"

"No."

"How can you not know him? He says you participated in the Salvadoran Revolutionary Student Front in 1974 and 1975; that you joined the PRTC in 1976, that you were part of the Liberation League, and that you've worked among students and peasants."

"That man lies! I don't know him."

"Nidia, he says he knows you. Remember Pablo Renan? Are you sure you don't know Mario Zetino? What year did you graduate from high school? What school or institute did you attend? So, what did you study at the university? Psychology? How far did you go?"

"I don't know!"

"'*I don't know, I don't know.*' How can you not know about your own life? It makes no sense your not being able to answer such elementary questions. Who recruited you? Why did you join the subversives? What made you leave your comfortable life, María Marta Valladares? When did you join?"

"I don't know! I don't know anything and I'm not going to say anything."

There was a long silence. Finally, I felt the need to defend myself. I began to explain how, as an adolescent, I became conscious of injustice and exploitation. How I started to teach people who were illiterate how to read and write. I was outraged by the misery in which the peasants are forced to live, but I didn't understand what was necessary to bring about change.

"Until you became a terrorist," someone interrupted. I ignored the comment and continued:

"At thirteen I knew nothing about politics. It was later, when I was seventeen and studying at the university, that I began to understand the reasons for the exploitation. I set out on my own to look for the way to end injustice."

"So, it was at the university that you became a terrorist?"

"No, I've never been a terrorist. By studying the real world somewhat more objectively, I found the explanations for what I had seen and experienced."

"Did you use the literacy manual? This one?" They removed

the blindfold and showed me the manual.

"No, not when I was with the nuns. I invented my own method which was nothing like this."

"The wagging tongues say that you studied at Divine Providence, and that it was there where you were brain-washed. And then?"

"And then, nothing! Nothing happened!" I shouted back."You say that you know my history, that Mario Zetino told you everything. So, why bother asking me?" There could be no doubt by then: they knew all about me.

"Lady, do you take us for idiots? We've studied and been trained for these investigations. We want *you* to tell us how your story began."

"I studied at Divine Providence. I graduated from there and in 1970 I started college. I concentrated my studies on two general areas, and later on psychology. In 1979 I married someone who was petit-bourgeois. I divorced him because he would not join the revolution. That's my story. It's that simple." I lied in order to hide the real identity of my child's father; he was a revolutionary like myself.

"We want to know about your participation in subversive struggle."

"You know who I am, where I was. You want me to confirm it? It won't come from me. You saw me at La Palma, you wounded me at the war front, you captured me there. What more do you want from me?"

"What were your responsibilities? What did you do? We want it all. *Everything!* You understand?"

Silence. I tried to blank them and their questions out of my mind. How many hours was the last interrogation? How long did this one last? Each stretch of questioning without interruption took about eight hours; there were three shifts every day. They came in by twos or fours, in staggered turns. Sometimes they were six. The captain was always there. Didn't he sleep either?

"Don't go to sleep! We're working," they shouted at me.

Their treatment of me and their techniques varied. They believed that they could soften me up, that they could break me. They used mostly psychological torture, but they also looked for ways to make my physical condition worse. I was already in bad

50

shape and getting worse.

"So, how do you feel?" someone sneered.

"How do you expect me to feel?"

"You must be all right. We've treated you well. We've treated you better than anybody else – like a queen!"

"I'm a prisoner of war."

"But, you've become difficult. Others have collaborated but you don't seem to want to help. For example, Guadalupe Martínez even fell in love with one of the guards. Don't you know that she had the guard's child? Then she wrote all kinds of bullshit in her book."

I stupidly fell for the provocation and screamed, "You know you're lying, you bastards!"

"And you, of course, will also write lies. Though I can't imagine why you would really want to play the heroine. Look, you say that you haven't even been to Cuba, while the other leaders lead the good life waltzing around the world. Look at Ungo,[1] look at Zamora,[2] enjoying the best hotels, traveling to Havana and Moscow, and here you are. Are you going to sacrifice your life for them? You've got to be kidding! They're not going to be able to do anything to get you out of here; you're the only one who can help yourself. It depends on how smart you are."

Blood rushed to my head, my adrenalin flowed. I felt that if they dared say all those things to me, who knows what they would tell the more humble *compas*. "So, I'm smart if I become a traitor?"

"Look, for instance, Mayo, from the political commission of the FPL,[3] he told us here that he'd been the one responsible for carrying out the massacre at Quebrada Seca.[4] You communists take no pity on us. Imagine, all those murders!"

"It's not true! You guys have such low morale you must twist

---

1. Dr. Guillermo Ungo, general secretary of the National Revolutionary Movement (MNR), and was president of the Democratic Revolutionary Front (FDR). Died early 1991.

2. Ruben Zamora, secretary general of the Popular Social Christian Movement (MPSC) and was vice-president of the FDR.

3. Popular Liberation Forces.

4. A bridge at KM82 of the Pan American Highway.

the truth in order to fool yourselves. The truth about Quebrada Seca is that your troops were giving themselves up, they were deserting en masse."

"And so you killed them."

"No, *you* did. In order to teach them a lesson: that they shouldn't surrender. You massacred and mutilated your own fallen soldiers. You had no respect for them! You tell them that if they give themselves up we will kill them. Yet we have freed everyone whom we have ever taken prisoner, soldiers and officers alike. We've handed them over to the International Red Cross. How different that is from what you do! Take the case of Janeth Samour. The only ones we have not handed over are those who have chosen to stay with us."

And so the hours went by. They would ask me the names of members or leaders of the FMLN. Did I know them, what did they do, where were they...? They would try to discredit the leadership, trying to get to me. They attempted to smear the character of *compañeros*, either those who were dead or those who had been prisoners before me and were released through FMLN actions. They wanted to destroy those examples that gave me strength. But we knew those *compas*, we knew their strength of character, their courage and revolutionary will. Their image could never be stained. They had earned our respect and the responsibility they carried. Ana Guadalupe Martínez, Mayo, Marcos, Galia, and Facundo[1] were all released because of heroic actions carried out by the FMLN. Revolutionary organizations never freed traitors from jail.

It was nothing but propaganda, like Quebrada Seca and other gruesome events that are blamed on us. The regime relied on fostering terror, insecurity, doubts. Psychological warfare aims at the emotional, not the rational. The slander and manipulation of the truth is intended to elicit a sense of rejection. They fear the surrender of their soldiers in battle, and therefore need to see prisoners waiver in their belief in victory and their trust in their *compañeros* so that they will talk. In this way they try to undermine the support for the FDR-FMLN among the civilian

---

1. Facundo Guardado, member of the leadership of the FPL. He participated in the negotiations at La Palma and Ayagualo and was the one who received the liberated prisoners on October 24, 1985.

population.

Crash! An interrogator suddenly interrupted my private thoughts by thumping the table. It infuriated me every time, but I didn't let on. One of them plugged in an electrical saw and ran it close by me and all around me. They wanted to make me afraid, to destabilize me, to break my resolve.

• Chapter 11 •

It was probably around noon on April 25 when they took me to the cell, pulled off the blindfold and threw me onto the mattress. The light bothered me, and thousands of thoughts went through my head at once. Why have they brought me here? The answer was a handshake. "I'm Major Aviles, from the Armed Forces' press office."

"Go away! I don't want anything to do with you."

"I've come from Teleprensa; I've come to interview you."

"Go away!" I put a towel over my face to block out the blinding light and turned towards the wall.

"You're insolent!"

He turned around and left. That day was the first time they allowed me to rest, but not sleep, for four hours. There was no doubt I was in a weak state. I was not eating very much, and at that point it had been almost twenty-four hours since I'd had anything to eat. I couldn't organize my thoughts. Exhausted, depressed and furious, I was a bundle of mixed emotions as I started to sing:

> With faith it's possible to dream,
> to fight without fear,
> to bear the pain,
> love unequaled beauty,
> and be ready to confront hell
> if duty so demands.
> I know that if I can always be
> faithful to my ideals
> I will always be

at peace in my life
until the end
as I know,
before me, others also held on
until the end
ever faithful to their ideals.

"Listen to her sing! Shut up!"

"Leave her alone!" said another.

I was seated. I was feeling worse and worse but I did not want to show it.

"What kind of work do you have going on in Berlín? In Salineras? How are the *Mardoqueo Cruz* commandos structured? Why do the guerrillas have it in for the police? Who passes information on to them? Where's Roberto Roca?[1] When does the FMLN General Command meet?" They knew I wasn't going to answer them, that I would tell them I didn't know. Why did they insist so?

I imagined a conversation with one of our dead *compañeros* who was saying, "The truth is that they really don't know; they expect you to break at any moment, die or go crazy, get muddled or run away screaming. They expect you to fall apart in some fashion. Yet they're the ones who lose control when they can't boost their morale by breaking you, and when they see you setting an example to others. Then they can't stand it any more and they kill you. You die while being tortured or they throw you out on the road, on El Playon or in the Lempa River. Imagine the terror in the faces of those humble folk who end up discovering the bodies. But this simply shows our strength, and our message. They know that we will die before betraying."

"Was that what happened to you?" I asked compassionately.

"Yes, of course."

"This woman's crazy. Nidia! Don't go to sleep!" someone yelled, interrupting this dialogue.

"I'm awake."

"You're dreaming. You didn't come here to sleep. But look, we'll let you sleep if you cooperate."

---

1. Roberto Roca is secretary general of the PRTC and a member of the General Command of the FMLN.

"No!"

The trumpet sounded reveille, and then there were footsteps. The sounds of a new dawn. They were dragging the chairs on the second floor of the interrogation section. Much later I would find out that Felipe Fiallos[1] was being held there at the time. And on the third floor was the traitor Miguel Castellanos. They had already broken him — something I never would have believed possible.

It was only those noises that let me know when day or night began. I had lost all sense of time in that place with the blindfold permanently covering my eyes. I didn't even know what day it was.

Maybe today is April 26 already, I thought. If that's the case, I'll dedicate it to the birthdays of my brother Rafael and Commander Camilo Turcios.[2]

My brother was born healthy but he had a fall when he was about a year-and-a-half and seriously injured the left side of his brain. He became intellectually disabled and later developed schizophrenic psychosis. He was first admitted to a psychiatric hospital when he was eleven years old. During the early years of his life our family didn't have sufficient money to pay for the treatment he required. Little by little, through my mother's efforts, he received different treatments – drugs, electric shock – which would make him better temporarily. In spite of his disability, he finished fourth grade. He was older than I by a year which was probably the reason that we were so close. We loved each other deeply. He used to say I was the sister he loved the best, for even when I joined the struggle I continued paying attention to him whenever possible, and I always worried about him. For me, he was almost like a son. In addition to the problems that we had at home, there were other factors that made his situation worse. They performed a lobotomy on him in 1973, which took away some of his aggressiveness. I was practically his nurse during that time. His life has been spent between home and the psychiatric hospital.

---

1. A member of the leadership of the FPL, captured in April 1985 and later freed in the prisoner exchange for Inés Duarte.

2. A commander of the PRTC and a member of its political commission.

Brother,
dear brother,
I think of you
and your thirty-four years
you and your childhood
you and your adolescence
youth and maturity
lost in the madness of time
trapped in psychosis
tangled in schizophrenia.
You, so pure and sweet,
so aggressive yet so gentle.
Child-man.
My mother's been there beside you
all your thirty-four years.
Your father,
our father, today far away
but still close to you
after seventeen years.

I wished that my brother had been able to lead a normal life. I wished he could have been a great combatant like Camilo Turcios, or simply, a normal human being. But reality was different. I loved them both very much.

Back in interrogation, they suddenly stopped firing questions, roughly grabbing my hands and rubbing them with a liquid. Then they forced my fingers on to a pile of papers; I resisted and one of them lifted my blindfold enough for me to see: they were cards for taking fingerprints.

The questions started again. I couldn't stand it any longer. It was all too intense.

"Who are the directors of the FMLN urban work?"

"What is the structure of the FMLN?" another asked. "How many fighters do you have? Who's going to take your place, Nidia? Where does the FMLN get its money? What is CIAS, DADPAZ? What is Z-0, Z-3, Z-5? When does AMES meet? What's the structure of the PRTC? Who's responsible for logistics? Isn't it José Juan? What is 'pliers,' 'hammer,' and 'crowbar'?"

One question after the other, together, in pairs, rolling over each other, or simply repeated with pauses in between. They took me away in the chair, past many corridors and doors.

"Here! What a mess you look, comb your hair."

"I don't want to! Why should I?"

• Chapter 12 •

They removed my blindfold in the Officers' Club. I was facing cameras. It was the national press. I couldn't concentrate well because of my physical condition and surprise. Nevertheless, I began to outline my case: "I was captured...in a commando-type operation carried out by Air Force troops led by a U.S. adviser who captured me...I was wounded by one shot in my shoulder-blade, one in my arm, one in my ankle, along with numerous splinters, another in my leg, as well as a burn on my arm. I am a prisoner of war.

"My interrogation has been cruel, enduring days and nights without sleeping. They have not respected the condition of my wounds or the stress. Despite medical recommendations for rest, the interrogations have been interminable.

"The day I was captured I was wearing olive green, with my hat and military equipment, just as you saw me at La Palma. Today I am here in this shirt, wounded, and blindfolded. But I still turn my face toward the sun. I can stay here for who knows how many years or perhaps they will shoot me. I have been fighting for my people for fourteen years so I am not afraid to die. They can send me to be killed, to be shot. But history, this history of our people, is written with fire and the sword. They can cut out my tongue, skin me, but I will never betray my people! Today my life enters a new phase, but as a revolutionary, wherever and however I am, I will never change my convictions. Because those ideas spring from the blood of my people and as long the roots of our struggle exist, so will the cause of our liberation."

The journalists were all taking notes. Their faces were tense. Fearful. Since announcing my capture, the military's press office had promised that I would make a statement, but now I was speaking my mind.

"The U.S. and Duarte don't want revolution," I continued. "They want war that leads to peace, the peace of the graveyard and secret prisons, of hunger and injustice. I am convinced that in order to have peace, it is necessary to struggle. Now is the time to struggle for what one day we will achieve. As Commander Facundo Guardado once insisted: 'Peace with justice. Peace is not won by begging, it is *conquered*.' We in the FDR-FMLN are sensible people; we are not militarists. We demonstrated this at La Palma when we sat down to face-to-face talks without our weapons, just as the FMLN General Command asked us to do. And if they asked me do to so again, for the sake of peace, I wouldn't hesitate for an instant. I believe a political solution to the conflict is possible, and not the military solution that the government and the Reagan administration are attempting to impose. That is why we proposed April 21 as the date for talks in Morazán. In the first round of talks we also proposed sitting down at the table.

"Now I am a prisoner of war. The war continues because our ideals continue. Whether or not Nidia Díaz exists, the people will triumph. The struggle will continue because the reasons for it still persist: poverty, hunger, exploitation, violation of human rights. But I believe a political solution is prudent and patriotic. We have no interest in prolonging the war. But that does not mean we are prepared to lay down our arms without an all-embracing and lasting solution."[1]

Finally! I was able to explain to the press many of things that I wanted to say. What freedom!

The officers stopped the meeting, calling back all the journalists. There were perhaps thirty of them. When they were leaving, their eyes looked to me, wanting to console me. There was one point during my speech when I faltered saying I really did feel quite ill. I noticed a journalist on the verge of tears; who could that have been?

That very night radio, television, and all the press gave extensive coverage to my statement. My mother saw my photo, sitting with my face turned upward with a very profound sadness. She read the newspaper commentaries which said that I appeared to be crazy. She became ill and had to be hospitalized. Poor thing!

1. These declarations appeared in the newsletter of a Salvadoran women's organization.

My mother didn't realize that I was in greater possession of my senses than ever before.

Once again, I was blindfolded. My head itched. The itching began to go up and down. Lice! It can't be! Yes, Nidia, another gift from the blindfold or comb to make your life even more unbearable. *Their* lice! This too you must overcome, I told myself.

Early in the morning they took me to Cell 20. It had been a terrible night. They had been close to bashing me. I wished they had, for then I would have spat on them. At times, they provoked me to do just that. The interrogator became furious when I called him an ignoramus. It was impossible to discuss anything with them. Would they never understand the reasons for our struggle?

They said that my mind had been clogged up from so much indoctrination. Actually, I felt sorry for them; most were from poor families and had sold their souls. Now they were in so deep they could not get out. They had murdered, tortured, committed open genocide; they knew that popular justice would catch up with them. That fear made them act increasingly with greater fury, more venom.

The detective and the interrogator were there, facing the long, thin mattress, watching me. Two women from the government's Human Rights Commission arrived. They promised to bring me clothing "even if it were theirs," they said. They seemed friendly and genuinely distressed by my circumstances.

Two nurses came to bathe and dress me with the clothing they had brought. The bath relaxed me and I ate a little. The International Red Cross came again. I gave them instructions on how to comfort my mother and to tell her that I was fine.

Again, the interrogators' questioning persisted. This time it was harder to resist as the bath and lying on the mattress made me sleepy. But they would never let up.

• Chapter 13 •

I couldn't talk anymore. I didn't have the energy. Now they were asking me a lot of simple things such as what music I enjoyed, what kind of food I liked, and so on. The third phase of the interrogation had started which involved an intense discussion of social problems. It seemed they were trying to probe my personality. It was incredible. We talked about everything: socioeconomic structures, alcoholism, poverty, prostitution. It seemed their aim was to exhaust me with talk and deprive me of sleep.

The interrogator kept at me. It seemed like a dialogue between lunatics, something totally incomprehensible. I told them that when we were victorious, we would take steps to get rid of prostitution, that women would no longer have to sell their bodies. One of them responded: "Oh, no! If there weren't whores, we would always be getting nice girls pregnant. Besides, it's a good business. I once owned a whorehouse. Each girl got paid forty colones and I kept a percentage. I don't like that business any more so I've gone into taxis. I earn more with taxis...Don't look at me like that! We all have businesses here. What do you think? Your needs grow and you have to make your future secure, lady. That's what life is all about these days."

"And that's why we want changes! You disgust me!" I told him. I was thoroughly repulsed by everything around me. Unable to make them leave, I had to endure them. Let lightening strike them! I wished. They were trying to exhaust me by their talking. I didn't want to listen. I turned my mind to the *compas*, the struggle, my son...

My thoughts escaped to one morning north of San Miguel, when some *compas* were breakfasting together. I was in my hut answering some messages and listening to the news. A burst of heavy artillery fire startled me. Without letting go of the cup of coffee I had just started to drink, I rushed outside to see what was happening. I couldn't determine where they were firing from when a missile whistled past me. I threw myself instinctively to the ground, spilling the coffee. I made it to the trench. I then heard the artillery fire further away. A few minutes later I was informed by radio that a 105mm missile had damaged the hut where we kept the medical supplies.

I wanted to see for myself what had happened. I told them I would try to reach the hut. I walked for half an hour. The *compas* had already separated the damaged medicines, about twenty percent of the supplies. The missile had landed behind the hut. In another hut, five *compas* were in the hammocks, two with malaria, one crippled, and two wounded.

"They're pretty wild, those sons of bitches," I commented. "This attack was in retaliation for our ambush and the thirteen they lost just ten hours ago on the Pan American Highway at Estanzuelas. I think the artillery pieces are on 'La Cancha'."

I stayed there about an hour. Some of them told me stories about their lives. As I was leaving, one of them, Raúl, said to me, "Commander, can you get us some guitar strings? Last night one snapped and we've written a song..."

"He's in love," explained one of the wounded *compas* with a wink. A few days later, I saw them again at a party. I still remember their smiling faces.

My mind was a whirlpool. Suddenly, I felt a hand around my throat, gently squeezing. I didn't flinch. It squeezed again. I held my breath, expecting more. It let go. Silence. I could feel his breathing.

"You were asleep!" the interrogator yelled as he hit the table.

"Don't shout at me!" I shouted back.

"Oh yeah? We're in charge here and you're going to have to put up with us, do you understand?"

"My plan worked, Nidia," one of them boasted. "You've been sent more papers. You can't deny these documents are yours." I heard him examine the stack of papers. "We're really hot stuff," he bragged. "Don't you agree?"

This was a new ploy to try to confuse me, to make me feel guilty, to weaken my resistance. Of course, it was ridiculous for them to think that I would have so many papers. Everything was a means to pressure me.

• Chapter 14 •

I was taken to the Officers' Club and put in front of cameras again. Some men identified themselves as journalists with a European news agency. They said they had been with Miguel Castellanos in the morning.

"With Miguel?" I asked.

"Yes, with Miguel. Do you know him?"

"No."

How had these journalists got to see Miguel, who had been my *compañero* in the struggle. I wasn't able to tell. They asked me several questions, all directed and pro-government. I answered them very carefully and confidently. I gave them no room for manipulation.

"Why are there desertions from the FMLN?" one of them asked.

I stared at him and queried, "What desertions? All that is part of the regime's propaganda. It's part of the psychological war."

"Commander Nidia, why doesn't the FMLN respect human rights?"

"Well, if you consider complying with the Geneva Accords and its protocols isn't respecting human rights, then you are viewing the world upside down. The FMLN has shown repeatedly that it respects prisoners of war. We've handed over to the Church all those captured in combat as an example of making the conflict more humane. We've given urgent medical attention to the wounded as far as we're able."

The questions then took a different tack. One of them asked how they were treating me.

"However it suits the regime," was my reply.

"Are they treating you well or badly?"

"I've already told you: however it suits the regime."

He was obviously an inexperienced interviewer. In prison, most of these interviews seemed tendentious and pro-government. Some journalists' questions were not impartial and provoked me into debates; at times they really harassed me. Why did I take the bait, under these conditions of confinement? My only concern was to help reach people with our true beliefs and objectives. I was afraid they were distorting or using my declarations for other purposes. It was always a risk. It was a learning experience which could prove costly.

Later, on the way back to my cell, I remembered my first interview in 1983 in the north of San Miguel. It was with a foreign reporter and I was underground. He was a progressive journalist and didn't know much about me. I always gave the urban front war reports using men's names because I didn't want it detected that one of its principal chiefs was a woman.

I was also interviewed at La Palma during the negotiations on October 15, 1984. We answered questions at the press conference we held after the meeting and then, in the same vein, gave some joint interviews. The journalists that day had had a difficult trip between Miramundo and La Palma, a distance of some ten kilometers. They arrived soaking wet from the rain, shivering in the cold, and were generally exhausted from the effort. They had to warm themselves around a camp-fire. Several journalists tried desperately to bring microphones and cameras into the church in La Palma. Here in prison, I had so far made two statements but the journalists asked no questions.

Now the opportunity of this interview had presented itself.[1] Back in my cell I wondered what the FMLN and the other leaders would think of what I had said. I didn't know if I'd be helping or hurting. It was not like being on the outside and preparing for the interview, having an up-to-date and global vision of what is happening and having others with whom to talk things over. Since La Palma I had to publicly assume responsibility. Me! Who never liked or wanted attention; now I found myself in the public eye with a duty to spread the truth about our struggle. I was never satisfied after an interview because I always felt I could have done better.

I was back in the cell blindfolded. Two detectives were standing in front of me. The cell was damp but I could feel the heat of the midday sun. My cell was next to the one used for questioning. Next to that were more cells; I wondered who might be imprisoned there. Everything was so silent I felt the shadow of the *compas* over me.

"How do you feel?" asked one of the detectives.

"Just fine."

"Here everyone has to play their part for everything to turn out okay."

"I'm doing my best."

I imagined their faces. They were young men, dressed in civilian clothes. On the street nobody would suspect they were part of all this horror. Years ago, detectives could be easily spotted. Now,

1. In the prison I gave a total of six interviews: two interviews to CBS, one to Venevisíon of Venezuela, one to Central Latina de Prensa, one to Pranss of Europe, and one to Agencia de Noticias of Guatemala.

they were trained and groomed in order to be less conspicuous. I could recognize them by their voices, the smell of their sweat, the sound of their breathing, their touch. How many had there been? How many more? Lots, all kinds: tall and short, white and dark, thin and fat, in plain-clothes and in uniform. My thoughts turned to the *compas*. I pictured them, so unflinching, so dedicated, so peaceloving, so gentle.

• **Chapter 15** •

With my head bowed and itching from the lice, in the white darkness of the blindfold that stretched before my eyes, the minutes felt like eternal centuries.

"Nidia, we're going to let you watch television. See how well we treat you, allowing you entertainment," remarked one of the officers. They removed my blindfold and set up a television for me. The news program was reporting the composition of the Legislative Assembly. Then Miguel Castellanos appeared, surrounded by journalists and Gerardo Chevallier, the deputy minister of information. Miguel was introduced as the repentant guerrilla. He was going to join the "democratic" process because changes had already taken place in El Salvador and therefore the guerrillas no longer had any reason to exist. He had surrendered!

But how was it possible? Political breakdown? Loss of confidence in victory? Treason! I realized that Napoleón Romero, Miguel's real name, had already shown weaknesses before his capture in Olocuilta, in the department of La Paz, on April 11, 1985. He had often tended to shirk responsibility, and showed signs of pettiness, selfishness, a lack of fraternal spirit; he didn't adapt well to collective living and had begun to place his personal safety ahead of the offensive against the regime. His behavior also revealed an appetite for notoriety. He already appeared distant, cold in his relationships with the *compas*. His most recent political statements reflected a loss of confidence in the people to achieve victory. The Popular Liberation Forces (FPL) had already noted this and tried to help him overcome his limitations and political weaknesses.

"So, what do you think?" they leered in my face.

"He's a rat! Bring me a lemon!"

"What for?"

"I'm going to throw up. You're bastards!"

"So he's a rat, eh? He's an intelligent man. He's more important than you. He thinks with his head, he's rational, logical, and a good politician."

"No, he's a rat!"

"Don't you want to see him? We'll bring him," they suggested sarcastically.

"No, I won't stand for it! And if you bring him, I'll tell the Red Cross you've tortured me in the worst possible way."

"We'll bring him now if you like."

"If you bring him, I'll kill him, so that will be the end of it."

I pictured him in front of me and kicking him in the groin. They wouldn't get away with this.

"Nidia, are you crazy? He's an intelligent man. Understand, he's smarter than you. You are the fool."

"Lies! He's an opportunist. His resentment and his hunger for power have led him to save his skin at any price. It is better to die with dignity than to live like he does. Yes, he'll live – but without honor or glory, repulsive, like a coward, like a worm, even worse than you."

They weren't going to bring Miguel. It was obvious they were afraid of what might happen if they did.

I wrapped myself in images of other *compas*. The face of Luis Díaz appeared before me. I felt Janeth's hand touch me, so white and small. The expression and bravery of all those loved and disappeared were there beside me in that cubicle. The thugs standing over me no longer existed, only the *compas*. This nightmare could not be real. Miguel, didn't the blood and courage of your leader matter? Did the resolve and tortured skin of your lover count for nothing? Or the selfless sacrifice of she who bore you? Those of us who together forged and built the foundations of our party and the struggle, those of us who have shed blood during this war, did it all count for nothing?

And what about the blood and pain of thousands of Salvadoran workers? Those who for centuries have been oppressed and exploited. Wasn't their pain and suffering real enough for you? You surrendered without facing the final battle with courage and dignity. Did you want to destroy what is irreversible, indestructible? Didn't you have faith in the enormous creative capacity of our people? Didn't being born, loving, and struggling matter to you? You should have died in an honorable battle. Your treason was a stab in the heart of your people, to the revolution. But in spite of such betrayals, our people move forward and decide their own destiny. In spite of you!

A voice shattered my thoughts. "Nidia, are you awake?"

"Yes, I'm awake."

"Don't you know that Miguel is on the political commission of the FPL? He's been chief of the capital, San Salvador, and involved for much longer than you. And according to Mario Zetino, you've only been a member of the PRTC since 1977. He's more important than you."

"The period of time or position doesn't matter! Or which organization you belong to, or whether you're a man or woman, or how old. All that matters is this moment, the one we're risking. That is where our dignity lies."

Didn't Clara Elizabeth[1], Gloria Palacios, Sonia[2], Ana María[3], Felipe, Juan Chacón[4], Polín[5], mean anything to you, Miguel? They did to me. They mattered right now, especially when we both found ourselves in the regime's clutches, in this ultimate test of fire. All of us, and those still to come, mattered to Luis, to

---

1. Founder of the FPL and member of its leadership, killed in combat in Santa Tecla on October 11, 1976.

2. Claudina Calderón, student leader and member of the FPL, disappeared in 1983.

3. Melinda Anaya Montes, second most prominent leader of the FPL, assassinated on April 11, 1983. She was an outstanding leader of the masses.

4. FPL leader, member of the leadership of the FDR, assassinated on November 27, 1980.

5. Peasant leader of the Salvadoran Workers Union and of the Popular Revolutionary Bloc who was assassinated.

Margarita Peña[1], to Felipe Ramos, to Iveth Castro[2], and to many others. For that reason, I am alive and we shall all live on in the memory of our people, in their history, in their blood and courage, in the echoing sound of their liberation. We shall live, and with dignity!

"Nidia!" roared one of the interrogators, pounding the table again.

"What do you want?"

"Miguel is smart. Look, he's recognized the FMLN's defeat, he's recognized that it's impossible for you to win the war. He sees that we're on the path to democracy, while you still cling to totalitarian ideas. No, don't touch the blindfold! Do you want to look at us?"

"No! I don't want to see you!" I felt dizzy, confused. All at once Miguel's face appeared before mine. You, Miguel, lost hold of the guiding thread of history. Your vision clouded over. Everything went dark and your sense of smell perceived only death. You were frozen in time and betrayed. Didn't you understand that time is on our side?

"Wake up!" another one shouted in my ear.

"Miguel is nothing but a dog in Reagan's service, he coils like a snake to Duarte, to the man who has destroyed El Salvador and who is greatest traitor of them all. He's a shit, just like all of you!"

"Hey, lady, you're out of your mind!" said one of the officers, somewhat taken aback by my vehemence.

Sometime later, Dr. Bottari, commenting on Miguel, said, "That one won't even be a trouble-maker," expressing the disdain of seeing one's adversary crumble. Miguel hadn't understood the source of our strength: the endurance and confidence in the future, the resolve to struggle for what one truly believes, the force of conviction up to the moment of truth, when death may surprise us.

I pressed my left hand against my forehead. I wanted to stop thinking...I started to sing:

1. Member of the FPL leadership, sister of Commander Felipe Peña Mendoza.

2. Gladis Meardi, a cadre of the PRTC, captured at a bus stop and disappeared in 1981.

Thanks to life
which has given me so much,
given me happiness
and given me tears.
Happiness and sorrow,
the two sources
for my song,
the song of my people
my own song.

"Shut up! We're working, not partying."
"Shut up yourselves! Why don't you go back where you belong," I answered in anger, and continued to sing.

• Chapter 16 •

How many hours had passed? I had no idea. The questions kept coming: Where is Salvador Guerra? Are you familiar with Chalatenango, Morazán, northern San Miguel, Usulután, Guazapa? Do you know Joaquín Villalobos?[1] Lucio? Where is Zamora? Mario González? Fernando Gallardo? Roberto Roca? Schafick Handal?[2] Facundo? Fermán?[3] Leonel?[4] So many names and faces, so many heroes were recalled in my mind. But I said nothing.

I remembered it was April 30, my father's birthday. The poor old man, he always wanted a better life. When I was seven years old, I rebelled against him after he beat my mother. He caused her so much suffering. She worked during the day as a secretary and also at night as a seamstress since her salary wasn't enough

1. Joaquín Villalobos is secretary general of the People's Revolutionary Army (ERP), FMLN commander, and a member of the FMLN General Command.

2. Schafick Handal is secretary general of the Salvadoran Communist Party, FMLN commander, and a member of the FMLN General Command.

3. Fermán Cienfuegos is secretary general of the National Resistance (RN), FMLN commander, and a member of the FMLN General Command.

4. Leonel González is secretary general of the Popular Liberation Forces (FPL), a commander of the FMLN and a member of the FMLN General Command.

to make ends meet. My father drank and gambled the money away. It took a lot of courage for my mother to leave him sixteen years ago.

This home life meant that I matured early, rejected all fantasies about marriage, and avoided attachment to material things. My father came from a well-off, landed family, and was educated at a private school and in the United States. He therefore had a petit-bourgeois view of the world, and was impressed by appearances and symbols of wealth. He was always acquiring things and then having them repossessed due to non-payment or else would have to take them to the pawnbroker. He had a modest house but wasn't satisfied because he wanted a large house. We always ended up out on the street because we couldn't pay the rent. We lived in fifteen houses in different neighborhoods.

Mainly due to my mother's encouragement, I received a scholarship to a Catholic school, from which I graduated. I studied hard in order to keep my scholarship. Those were difficult times. My mother even pawned her dresses and wore ripped-up shoes. It was not a happy home. Later, I came to understand, both socially and emotionally, my father's behavior. I used to visit him when I could, though I haven't seen him for many years now.

I knew his other children and when I could do something for them, I did. I have no regrets, I never turned my back on him. I am sure these experiences in my childhood and adolescence contributed to my developing a social conscience. From the time I was young, my relatives recalled that I was always giving away my toys and food to children who were without, and that I never liked frilly, ostentatious dresses. My mother helped organize several community libraries, among them a children's library, which motivated me to read. I read mostly stories and fantasy. I loved Jules Verne. His books created a fantastic world for me that contrasted with the harsh reality of my home. I mixed with children and young people of all kinds in these libraries, mostly those from poor areas.

My mind was elsewhere when a nurse approached me and thrust a glass of water into my hands. "Take this pill, it's a sedative," she ordered.

My fingers touched it, it wasn't a regular pill. I lifted the blindfold slightly and recognized the small, blue, diazepan. "No!

No, I don't want it! Take it away!" The pill was intended to make me more tired, but they would not let me sleep.

• Chapter 17 •

I heard shots ring out through the darkness. Where could they be coming from? Who or what were they firing at? It seemed to be a ruckus of some kind. But at this time of night? Perhaps it happened every night but I hadn't noticed it before. It could also be part of their psychological torture. I had a bitter taste in my mouth, it felt dry and pasty. Horrible. I hadn't brushed my teeth for days. I was getting used to the loss of personal routines. It was all a question of survival.

> Arise ye workers from your slumbers,
> Arise ye prisoners of want.
> For reason in revolt now thunders,
> And at last ends the age of cant.
> Now away with all your superstitions,
> Servile masses arise! Arise!
> We'll change forthwith the old conditions,
> And spurn the dust to win the prize.
> Then comrades come rally,
> And the last fight let us face.
> The International
> Unites the human race.

I repeated those verses in my mind as I sat there in prison, our fifth war front – what we jokingly called "Pedro Pablo Castillo." It was now May 1, May Day, the international workers' day. The May Day Committee had called for a large demonstration. This committee was composed of the Workers Solidarity Coordinating body, which was formed by government employees, laborers, and the urban poor. The National Waterworks Administration union had also joined the strike.

"Nidia! Wake up! Don't fall asleep!" they said.

I noticed that a new shift of interrogators had come on. I didn't recognize the voices. They had foreign accents, but they weren't North Americans. A few nights before, I had overheard a Yankee having a lengthy discussion with my interrogators. They hadn't wanted the U.S. advisers to participate directly in the interrogation, but I knew they were there, guiding those who were questioning me. This voice was Latin American, Venezuelan. The other voice was familiar to me, very familiar. It sounded like Vides Casanova, the defense minister.

"Nidia, we haven't come to interrogate you. We've come to have a little chat with you," said the Salvadoran official.

"We're government advisers, not interrogators," said the Venezuelan.

What nerve! I thought. "OK, if you want to discuss things with me, why don't you remove my blindfold so we can see each other face to face, like at La Palma? What do you want to discuss?" I challenged.

"We can't take off your blindfold; you're a prisoner. We want to discuss the negotiations with you. We don't think the FMLN is sincere. Besides, you should know that several of your camps have fallen: Nueva Estrella, Mala Cara, Siempre Viva."

"I don't believe anything you say. You think you can demoralize me by telling lies."

"Well, you're going to have to believe us. There was heavy fighting and Jorge Rivera, Modesto Aguilar, and Ovidio all died. Camilo Turcios is already dead and Miguel Mendoza has replaced you. Ana and Mario also died in Guazapa, and we've captured quite a few others. The FMLN hasn't got a chance, they're defeated and your party is finished, split, and everyone blames you. They consider you a traitor and have disowned you."

"Nidia, the government would be very willing to send you to recuperate in another country, Switzerland, Finland or Australia, and then bring you back," said one of the advisers.

"No thanks. I will only leave under orders from the FMLN General Command. Otherwise, I don't move."

"Don't be like that. But don't get your hopes up because you won't be allowed to leave. The president might have very good intentions, but the Armed Forces won't agree. So you're going nowhere," they sneered.

Obviously I was to remain yet another victim of the Salvadoran Armed Forces who do not recognize the right of those wounded in battle to receive adequate medical attention or be released to receive such treatment. They arrogantly ignore the international treaties on these matters because doing so would mean recognizing the fact that there are two forces, two armed forces, fighting for power in El Salvador. Thus, from the political standpoint, they can never admit it; and militarily they hope to impede our mobility and lower the morale of our movement.

"Miguel Castellanos wants to see you," said the official, trying another tack.

"No! Listen, I don't want to see him!" I shouted at them.

"Are you afraid of him?"

"No, I'm not afraid. Besides, if you wanted to, you would have already brought him. I'm your prisoner, you don't have any reason to consult with me first."

"OK, tell us, if the proposal for negotiations is genuine, what is the proposal? What is the peace proposal? What have been the advantages for the FMLN and the FDR in the talks?"

The questions were direct, blunt, and well-formulated. It was clear they were not regular interrogators. "How would you, or you and your people, describe the position and performance of each member of the delegation who went to the talks at La Palma?" the official asked. "How did Vides Casanova, for example, handle himself?"

The interrogators had obviously already reported that I had commented that Vides Casanova and Duarte, during the talks at La Palma, were for the truce. I emphasized this in order to exacerbate the contradictions among them.

"Vides Casanova hardly said a word," I answered calmly. "He said that Duarte had already said everything there was to say."

"What do you think would be the composition of the two armies? Why do you want to dissolve the security forces?"

"As you already know, we believe only one army should exist in El Salvador, based on a negotiated settlement. The government of broad participation that would take office would represent all the sectors of our country. A single army would be established with the most honest officers and soldiers together with the revolutionary forces."

"So you already have resumes of all the members of the armed forces?" asked the other.

"Well, yes. Those who have abused power, like Bustillo, Ochoa, Staben, Vargas, and others, will be tried. In fact, they're already being tried. We have files on each one of you, we've studied you and know all about your backgrounds. In addition, we will dissolve the plans and structure of the current repressive bodies and build ones that will safeguard social order.[1]"

"Do you think Joaquín Villalobos will place himself under the orders of Vides Casanova?"

"It's not a matter of who will give orders to whom. Besides, experience has proven that Commander Villalobos is more capable than Vides to lead and carry out the war."

"You're joking!" he laughed. "Your ranks can't match ours. You don't even have *officers!*"

"What is this 'government of broad participation'? What is its program and its immediate reforms? Look, Nidia, you don't have an objective government plan. We've already studied your documents, but we want you to explain them to us."

"Here, under these conditions, I'm not going to talk. I will talk when there are more negotiations, face to face and without a blindfold. But not like this."

"Why do you carry out political executions among yourselves? What is the point of infiltrating the Armed Forces? Are there a lot of infiltrators? Why do you continue fighting if the government has already changed and human rights are already being respected? Look how we're treating you," said one of the advisers.

I wanted to laugh. "So why has the 1979 Proclamation of the Armed Forces which calls for reforms been stalled and blocked?" I asked. We had participated in the first government junta but were forced to resign our positions when the junta fell under the control of the right wing and increasingly served the interests of the United States.

I reiterated that the FMLN was not for dragging out the war, that we didn't want to see any more loss of human life or further

1. This was one of our positions in 1984-85, which in 1986, was more clearly defined. When a broad-ranging government takes office that has the participation of all the sectors that support a political solution among Salvadorans, a cease-fire will be agreed to. This transitional government will initiate a democratization process and call for free, honest and representative elections. The resulting government will take measures to establish one army.

destruction of our country's scant resources. I explained that we didn't want any businesses going bankrupt or further infringement on our national sovereignty to the point of an invasion by U.S. troops. But neither the Armed Forces nor the Reagan administration wanted a political solution and instead were stepping up the war, forcing us in turn to respond militarily. It is the social-economic and political crisis in El Salvador which had created refugees, unemployment and poverty.

We then argued about the contradictions among themselves, between the army and the U.S. advisers running the war. They pointed out the role of the middle class and questioned the unity within the FMLN, the alliance with the FDR and the FMLN's political-military strategy. They insisted over and over again that democracy reigned in El Salvador.

Many hours passed; my cracked lips burned. I found that the most difficult discussion I had on the principles and substance of our objectives. I simply repeated everything we had always openly published about our goals in the struggle.

"And if you showed up dead wrapped in the flag of the FMLN, what do you think public opinion would be? Don't you think they'd believe it was the FMLN?" they said again.

"Is that how you're planning to kill me? No one would fall for it!"

"What do you think about the Church? What is the FMLN's relationship with the Church?" one of the advisers asked.

"We have the same relationship that our people have with the Church. Our people are Christian. We deal with the Church hierarchy through an intermediary. You saw him yourselves at La Palma and Ayagualo, Monsignor Rivera y Damas. We hand over our war prisoners to him as a representative of the Church."

Questions, questions, more questions...

• Chapter 18 •

The interrogation finished at 5:30 a.m. I was very weak. They had tried to convince me, persuade me, break me. I gently leaned my head on the desk. My entire body hurt – my lips, my bones, my back, my ankles, my arms, the lice. It was unbearable. I only saw white darkness. My eyelashes pressed against the blindfold but I knew that the detectives were there. I grabbed the towel they had given me and I threw it on the floor. I tugged on the blindfold and adjusted it. I lifted myself strenuously up from the desk and dragged myself down to the floor. There I rested, but every few minutes they shouted at me not to fall asleep because some men were coming soon and I had to be awake and sitting up.

This was the third time they had let me throw myself on the floor to rest, if only for half an hour. It was time for the interrogators' change of shift. It seemed to me they were leaving slightly before their eight hours were up. Perhaps they were going out to get something to eat. They exhausted themselves more than I did, and were getting nowhere. A few times I stood up and leaned my wounded leg on the desk. One of the interrogating officers came in and found me in that position and demanded I take off the blindfold.

I took it off and looked at him. I recognized his voice. He had been questioning me at least once a day. I looked at him curiously.

"Look at you! And we broke Miguel so quickly, so easily," he remarked.

"You tortured him," I replied.

"No, we didn't torture him. We only talked to him." He watched me. His eyes filled up with tears. How strange is human emotion! And yet at the other times, when he was yelling at me, didn't he feel pity then? This incident remains in my mind.

After they finished the interrogation period, I would recognize him every so often, during inspection of the guards, or when he was taking back prisoners after an interrogation.

At noon, I was taken from my cell and brought to the Officers' Club where there were some journalists. The Red Cross had visited me that day and given me clean clothes which my mother had sent. They said the journalists were from the *Central Latina de Prensa*. From their questions I could tell they were pro-government and I thought they were trying to take advantage of me, hoping I would make a mistake and say something they could use, even if only a single word. They wanted to present me as a traitor. Their questions were different from the previous occasion, but were still on the same track:

"What do you think of the efforts to make the conflict more humane? Why do you shoot soldiers after capturing them? Why do you keep prisoners of war and why are there desertions among your ranks? To what extent do the documents that were captured with you hurt the FMLN? Will the PRTC become weaker due to your capture?"

The same questions the interrogators asked! I felt angry.

"What do you think of Miguel Castellanos?"

"He's a traitor," I responded sharply.

"After everything that has happened to you, what has hurt you the most?"

"That the work documents that I was careful with were captured. And the betrayal of Miguel Castellanos," I replied.

That sentence, together with my picture, was plastered all over television by the Armed Forces' press office.

Once again they asked me about my treatment in prison. "It's not a matter of answering good or bad. They treat me however they choose, whatever suits their purposes," I replied.

That afternoon, they took me to Cell 20, blindfolded and seated. The Venezuelan advisers came again and one of them commented on how dark the cell was, and ordered a light switched on. They began accusing our movement of many crimes. I vehemently argued that this was also part of their psychological war. The FMLN was doing everything possible to make the war more humane. "Aren't they treating you well? You see, things are already changing!" they said.

"OK, so why don't you tell me where Janeth Samour is," I answered.

"Why are you a commander? Why did they choose you to go to the first round of talks, but not the second? What is the criteria for determining your political cadre?"

The same questions over and over. That afternoon they brought along photographs from the negotiations. "Do you recognize this person?"

"No, I don't know him."

"You must know him. He also attended the first talks."

"Well, I don't know him."

"But you must know him. And this other one?" he almost screamed in his frustration.

The advisers left and the regular interrogators remained, assaulting me with their questions. I was anxious for the night to finish. I knew that the fourth and final phase of the interrogation was coming to an end, and that only twenty-four hours remained.

"I have to urinate."

One of them went out and brought back a pan. They were tired of carrying me to the latrine. But this way they had to dispose of my urine which angered them. However they had no other choice.

The police physician came in the morning. He came by frequently to see if they were taking care of me. Several times he told the interrogators to let me rest, but they had no intention of doing so. Their aim was to drive me to absolute exhaustion in order to break me. That morning my lips were completely cracked. I couldn't stand the thirst, the pain was unbearable. It had been one of the most stressful and exhausting nights. They hadn't allowed me to respond; there was only question after question.

"Why did you go to Mexico? Is it true you went there in 1982? That's what your passport says. When does the PRTC central committee meet? Where?"

They showed me six immigration cards with the same surnames as mine and asked me which was mine. They were confused. Strange coincidences, I thought, because none were actually mine.

> Love and strength
> confidence in the future
> the unshakable belief
> in battles to be won
> where do these come from?
> From firm convictions
> and strength in these convictions.
>
> And in that most difficult moment
> when death comes to surprise us,
> to warn us?
> We must confront it

with all the love and courage
rooted within
love and courage
that makes the enemy quiver,
tremble and surrender
in his own empty burrow.

P.N. May/85

Part Three

I survive
and reencounter
the sun

• Chapter 19 •

The climax of the interrogation had arrived. It was mid-morning when a second lieutenant with pale eyes entered. "Sign here!" he ordered, thrusting a paper into my hands.

"What is it?"

"An extrajudicial document."

"You want me to sign something without reading it?"

"You've had plenty of time. Now sign!"

I was angry. "I won't!"

"It's not a question of whether you agree or not. You have to sign."

"You can't force me. How dare you say here that when I was asked if I wanted an attorney I declined. You're trying to say the Church supports the FMLN and you want me to put that in writing! Your entire history of me is inaccurate — it's your lies and those of Mario Zetino."

The second lieutenant looked at me with anger burning in his eyes. He turned on his heels and left. They continued the questioning until the second lieutenant returned with another official holding another document in his hand. He read it to me and then asked: "Do you agree with this or not?"

"I already told you that I will not sign any document or paper."

"You have to sign this. If not, you will make things much harder for yourself."

"It doesn't matter. I won't sign anything."

Once again, he left furious. The interrogation recommenced. I sensed they were getting desperate: so many questions, so much violence in their voices. Now there was only one interrogator. He was called out of the room and didn't return.

A little while later they took me back to my cell where representatives of the International Red Cross arrived. I told them how I was and how they were treating me. Then I was taken back to the room to continue the interrogation. Later I was taken out again. The government's Human Rights Commission arrived and like the Red Cross, enquired about my health.

It was almost noon when the second lieutenant, another officer, a secretary, and two detectives came in. They brought a table, a typewriter, a desk, and a chair. Yet another document was placed in front of me and they asked: "And now, you won't sign? These people are witnesses to your conduct and all the investigations we've carried out."

I sat down on the mattress, looked at them and answered: "I've already told you I won't sign. I don't believe in this charade. How can you say that these people are civilian witnesses if they're *your* people? Besides, as a matter of principle, I'm not signing any document even if it only has my name on it."

They looked at one another anxiously and left. However, before leaving, the second lieutenant threatened me saying, "You'll regret this."

It is common practice for *compañeros* under interrogation and whose capture has been acknowledged by the government to be forced to sign an extrajudicial document. Thus the intelligence sections of the political police and army get a piece of evidence they can then use in the courts, beginning with the First Judge of Military Instruction. This document is presented in the newspapers, as well as on television and the radio, along with photographs. It serves as evidence that, in their view, legalizes arbitrary arrests. They force the prisoners to sign while blindfolded and don't allow them to read what they sign. But there have been compatriots, such as Felipe Fiallos, who refused to sign, as I did.

My thoughts were interrupted by the presence of several police, among them one nicknamed "Chiquitón," who lifted me up. They were all armed. "Collect everything you've got!"

They carried me outside to a waiting vehicle. I raised my blindfold and caught a glimpse of part of the National Police Headquarters buildings. I initially thought they were taking me to the women's prison of Ilopango and was overcome with happiness at the thought of being reunited with my *compañeras*. However, within moments I began to fear that the journey may have another destination and that this night might be my last. I began to fear they might be planning to do away with me in a death squad type action. I sensed it in their attitude and the expressions on their faces. So this was it! I thought. Nevertheless, they would never win, I reassured myself. I had no doubt that our people's struggle would eventually triumph.

For whatever reason, the vehicle never started. "Get out!" shouted the lieutenant. What had happened? I was sure a counter-order, probably by the Military High Command, had been made to keep me in jail and place me in isolation.

• Chapter 20 •

I allowed the hours to slip by while I kept my eyes fixed on the springs of the bunk above me. I wondered if they would let me out again for interrogation. I could smell my own sweat. It had again been a week since I had been allowed to take a bath. I couldn't stand the itching of the lice, which had been multiplying, and ran back and forth across my head. What a great time they were having, and I couldn't do anything because I couldn't move my right hand. I wished I could pick them out, but I didn't have that kind of dexterity in my left hand. I watched the shadows of dawn gradually illuminate the sadness of the place.

Some time later, one of the aides came in with breakfast. "Are you going to eat?" he asked.

"No."

"So how are you feeling?"

"How do I feel? How do you expect me to feel?"

My anger at that stage prevented me from making any distinction between my captors, between the interrogators and detectives, jailkeepers, aides, administrators, nurses, and doctors. They were all the same to me.

I began to retrace in my head the entire course of the interrogation: what I had said, what I had answered, what they had asked me. I wondered what would have happened if I had come up with some better answers, if I had chosen not to even open my mouth. Had I given anything away? No, I didn't think so. I had survived. I had won.

It was May 4. Colonel Melara Vaquero, a military judge,

arrived. He informed me that my case was under his jurisdiction and that, under orders from the minister of justice, Julio Samayoa, I was to remain temporarily at the National Police Headquarters. He said that the jail at Ilopango was not a safe place for me and that they would be looking for another.

"Why isn't it safe?" I asked. "The regime should guarantee my safety here or anywhere. I have completed the fifteen-day questioning period and should be transferred to Ilopango or to the women's prison."

"My dear Nidia, the regime cannot guarantee your safety there. You must understand there are groups of the right and the left in this country that the government does not control," said the colonel.

I was overwhelmed by a sense of fear. I realized he was referring to the interrogators, the political police, the chiefs' of staff intelligence service, the Military High Command, and the death squads. At any moment any of them could have planned to take me out and assassinate me, just as they had hinted during the interrogation. Was that why the regime could not guarantee my safety at Ilopango, or any other place?

"I don't accept that I must stay here," I responded. "You have to guarantee my rights wherever I am. You are obliged to carry out the international human rights accords."

"It's not a question of whether or not you agree. I'm telling you that you will remain here. I am complying with my responsibility to inform you, to let you know what the instructions are. Please sign here to acknowledge that you have been duly notified."

"Well, I'll sign that I am aware that I'm being held by the National Police, that the interrogation phase is over and that the intelligence services can't bother me any longer." At that moment, I did not understand that their admitting they couldn't guarantee my life at Ilopango was part of the psychological pressure they were constantly exerting upon me.

I could feel in my bones the dampness of the cell; the humidity of the dawn infused the entire cell, reaching into every corner. I had never felt so steamy. There were two windows on each side of the door, and a little vent above it; all of them had bars, thirty-two in total. On the far side of the cell was a little room with the latrine and a wash basin.

I needed to rest, to recover my strength. But I could not sleep. I wondered if all those days without sleep meant I would never sleep again. I desperately needed to get away from the sound of the interrogations taking place around me. I felt only through sleep could I escape.

All the political prisoners being held there were tortured physically and psychologically. Some of them went mad. Kidnapped in the city or the mountains, you were never told where you were going, and no one ever identified themselves. Depending on circumstances and on what they thought about you, you were then handed over to the political police for questioning, a process which took a minimum of two weeks. This procedure had been legalized by Decree 50, part of the permanent state of emergency and extended month to month since 1980. Paradoxically, this decree contradicted the regime's own constitution, which limited the interrogation period to three days, and prohibited any long periods of sleeplessness and blindfolding of the detained.

Sometimes they allowed you to sit down, but most of the time they kept you standing until you fell. I remember that in 1983 Commander Galia collapsed twice and she was beaten just like everyone else. First she was held in a secret jail, until they decided to send her to the National Police Headquarters. The most common method used in El Salvador has been to simply disappear people.

In prison you lost all notion of time: days and hours ran together. The interrogators were aggressive and abusive. They yelled at you. They hit the furniture, the doors, your body. They sent electric shocks through your body as you suffocated inside a strangling dark hood. The regime's most recent policies, in fact, tended to institutionalize this terror, to legitimize it.

In such "legal" interrogations they applied many different kinds of torture. In order to extract the truth or corroborate their speculations they used lies or half-truths hoping you would fall for them. The ultimate objective was to break your spirit, to make you feel alone, guilty. They promised that they would pardon you, that your family would be unharmed, and that your sentence would be reduced. You had only to pay the price of betrayal.

I kept seeing the detective leaning on the door frame. I thought of the officer who had tears in his eyes when he told me

Miguel Castellanos had been broken by talk alone. How could it be possible? This was one of the most painful blows I had to bear.

The prison was quiet. I could no longer hear the interrogations, but their echoes played in my head. I remembered the voice of the man who had said, "Look at me, Nidia. Never forget me. The FMLN is going to win. Remember me." How absurd! What went through my head at the time? I thought it was a trap. And the words of a certain lieutenant, after I had been singing during interrogation: "Nidia, you are unique." I began to understand more and more. Since their words had not broken me, I knew they were going to continue to harass me in one way or another.

• Chapter 21 •

It was dawn in my homeland. I pictured the newspaper vendors out in the streets, helping to disseminate ideas which were not their own. A trumpet played reveille. "Hut...two...three...," the police were marching. I could barely perceive the light of day through the cracks in the wall. Although I could not see it, I could feel it, touch it. I was alive.

For decades our people had struggled against the military dictatorships of Martínez, Aguirre, de Lemus, Sánchez Hernández, Molina, Romero. And now we were fighting against the Duarte dictatorship. This time the United States had been more astute and had legalized the terror: since 1980 60,000 Salvadorans, non-combatants, had been killed; there were about 6,000 disappeared, and a further 6,000 had been political prisoners. At that time there were more than 500 political prisoners in the country's legal jails — with more arrested every day. Even though eighty-five percent of these were workers, not guerrillas, they were equal victims of the indiscriminate repression.

It had been more than five years of great effort and continual sacrifice. El Salvador was now split between two forces, two powers — the FMLN and the Duarte regime. This was now an undeniable fact recognized both in the political-military arena as well as in international diplomatic circles. This duality of power was evident within the population, the countryside, and the social life of the country. On the one hand, there was a backward force, a power which was no longer viable and dying a slow death; and on the other, there was a new, vibrant, popular force, a progressive power which was growing stronger day by day. The FDR-FMLN was increasingly recognized by our people and other governments as a truly representative force, with a serious political program — the only force capable of resolving the serious national crisis. This was why Duarte, under pressure from the international spotlight on my case, felt obliged to acknowledge my capture.

Duarte needed some proof to show the U.S. Congress and other governments that human rights were now respected in El Salvador. I simply happened to be a convenient example for him. In addition, the U.S. Congress had come under pressure from different individuals and solidarity committees to make any aid granted to El Salvador conditional on an improvement in the human rights situation. Duarte's propagandists before the international community needed to rebuild the prestige lost by his government on this issue. To be able to present me as "wounded and captured" in this context was useful to the Military High Command. But it was something they would come to regret, because I had survived. Furthermore, they had not succeeded in breaking me.

There were already many organizations in El Salvador fighting for the respect of individual and collective human rights, for political and social freedoms: the non-governmental Human Rights Commission, the Committees of the Mothers and Relatives of the Disappeared, and the Committee for Political Prisoners in El Salvador. All of them had achieved many humanitarian victories.

There were also "neutral" humanitarian organizations such as the Legal Aid office which was part of the archbishop's work, a similar Christian Legal Aid, and the International Red Cross. The government had been pressured also at the international level by groups such as the International Federation for the Rights of Man, Amnesty International, Americas Watch and the World Court in the Hague. In November 1984 a conference on human rights was held at which more than 300 delegates, representing 113 humanitarian groups, condemned the Duarte regime.

It was the struggle of my people and the international pressure that allowed me to survive. But the key was really the grassroots movement. I owed nothing to the regime, absolutely nothing. My life was not a gift from Duarte, nor the Yankees. It was the result of the blood shed by my people.

On April 20 a three-hour meeting took place in Panama's Hotel Capitalino. Participating in the meeting were Salvador Samayoa and Mario Aguiñada from the FMLN and a high-ranking officer from the Salvadoran Armed Forces. It was only the second occasion that a meeting of this level had taken place.

The FMLN representatives insisted that there be a public acknowledgement by the Armed Forces of the capture of Janeth Samour, Miguel Castellanos and myself. They explained that the FMLN had always publicly acknowledged its capture of Armed Forces personnel. If the Armed Forces wanted a "dirty war" then that is what they would have, the FMLN representatives declared. They gave the Armed Forces twenty-four hours to make a statement. The next day the press office of the Armed Forces for the first time publicly acknowledged my capture.

I began to discover a world I had not previously known existed. It was all new for me. People came from France and the United States to visit me, something I could never have before imagined. One afternoon, when I was taken to the registration office, I had visits from several North Americans: Karen Parker, a doctor of law in the human rights field; Drs. Kimball and Gossi, from the University of San Francisco; Father Jose M. Moyet, president of the Ecumenical Committee of San Francisco and of the California Bishop's Conference. A French woman, Fabien Eleanor, of the International Federation for the Rights of Man, was also there to see me.

All these visitors lifted my spirits and informed me that they were aware of my physical condition; they were there to let me know I would be operated on in two weeks. They gave me a notebook, pens, and pencils and a book containing the Geneva Convention and its protocols. I could not believe my eyes! I felt so happy to experience first-hand what people-to-people solidarity means.

"Good morning, Nidia," said the guard as he brought in my breakfast.

"I don't want to eat."

"You know, we're all afraid of you because of the terrible way you look at us — as if we were your enemies. We're not all the same, some of us work here out of need."

I looked at him with surprise, and I also looked at the detective who, as always, was there watching me. It's true they didn't all play the same roles, but they were all part of the same game. "You are my enemies and I am a prisoner of war."

He was a young man of about twenty-two. He looked straight at me and then bowed his head. He was silent for a while and then left, saying on the way out, "Someday you'll understand that we're not all the same."

"Hey!" I said. "You don't all act the same, but all of you contribute to the same thing."

Later, feeling calmer, I began to observe them and to consider this question. The FMLN always pointed out that individual members of the army and police didn't all act the same, and that within that weave of interconnecting threads there was not only a division of labor, but a system of different ranks and levels. Besides, there were different individual motives of those who chose to remain part of the regime, depending on their origin and social standing, and according to their politics and personality. But, by their acceptance of the objectives of the Armed Forces, the great majority could be considered accomplices and participants — except, of course, those who were on the inside carrying out a mission for us.

In my case, the jailers, detectives, and administrative personnel conducted themselves according to their instructions. They were trying to improve the image of the regime. I had already observed sympathetic gestures from some of them who hoped to guarantee their future safety by acting in such a way so that I would not condemn them.

Commander Nidia Díaz leading a column of FMLN guerrillas

Nidia Díaz in an FMLN camp, 1985

Nidia Díaz

Commander
Nidia Díaz,
Morazán,
May 1984

En Policía Nacional está presa Nidia Díaz

Nidia Díaz se estaba peinando cuando ayer al mediodía tuvimos oportunidad de verle personalmente en un pasillo de la Policía Nacional. Morena, pelo liso, de un metro sesenta centímetros, de mirada profunda, como de meditación.

Para peinarse, usaba la mano izquierda, pues en la derecha tiene una lesión de bala o quebradura, supuestamente sufridas hace pocos días cuando fuera sorprendida por disparos en un enfrentamiento con efectivos del Ejército. La mano la muestra vendada.

El único movimiento que hacía con la mano derecha, era sostenerse la cabellera que ella se peinaba, y por momentos, la impulsaba hacia su rostro, de manera que no se le veía.

Luego dejaba la cara al descubierto, miraba profundamente hacia el techo, y en ningún momento vio fijamente a nadie de las

—Pasa a la página 21—

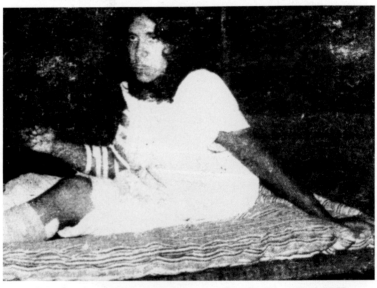

Salvadoran press report on capture of Nidia Díaz, April 1985

FDR–FMLN delegation address the people during negotiations with the Salvadoran government at La Palma, October 15, 1984. To the right is Nidia Díaz.

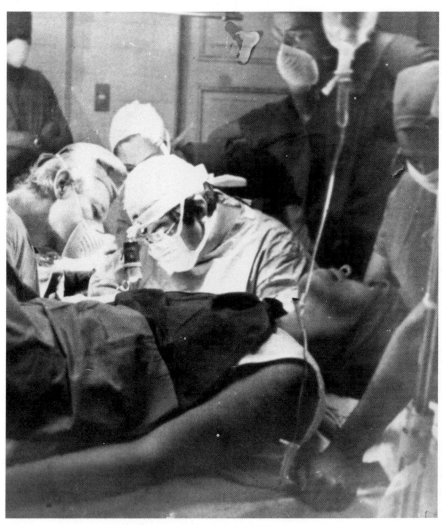

Nidia Díaz undergoing operation four months after her capture

Arriving Havana airport,
October 25, 1985

FMLN delegation, San José, 1990

Signing agreement with Salvadoran government on human rights during negotiations, San José, July 1990

Press conference, San José negotiations, September 1990

• Chapter 22 •

I didn't know what was wrong with me. I could only sleep for a couple of hours. I drank sugar water, but still couldn't sleep. I was still recovering from the sixteen days without sleep. For six days after the interrogation period I could not sleep at all, not even a minute. Finally when I was able to sleep for a couple of hours, I was awakened violently by the sounds of interrogations taking place next to my cell. "Who were you with? Answer me!" the interrogator was screaming. I could hear blows.

"What, can't you hear, stupid? Get up, get up! Let's see if you can stand up."

I didn't know what time it was. It must have been early morning.

The day before they had put a padlock on the cell. A detective was posted outside. It was a good day: I was pleasantly surprised to see María Julia Hernández, the representative of the archbishop's Legal Aid Office. She had come to see me six days after my capture and had only been able to explain where she was from and to wish me good luck. I had not answered her; I had been too surprised. They took me out of the interrogation cell block to the Officers' Club.

On this occasion we were able to talk more. She explained my legal situation, and told me that Legal Aid would have an attorney assigned to my case. At that time, they visited all the political prisoners at Ilopango and Mariona on a weekly basis. In my case, they would now come once a week to National Police Headquarters.

Dawn arrived, announced by reveille and the marching feet. The interrogation next door had finally ceased. It was May 10. My lunch was better that day, probably the same as the officers' food. I had not wanted to eat before, but this looked good – perhaps because it was Mother's Day. I ate, thinking that my mother should have received my letter by now.

Dearest Mother,

How painful it must be for you to see your daughter in such difficult straits – to have your mother's heart so torn. Mother, please do not worry. Understand your daughter is ready to give her life for her people.

They wounded me, they nearly destroyed me physically, but understand they never broke me, they never broke my morale. I've won the battle, and I will continue to fight, until my heart stops beating, until final victory.

Don't cry this May 10 for you or for me. Remember that you will always be my mother. Better times will come: a time of victory and fulfillment. But we will have to live through these difficult times first and maybe you and I might not survive.

Mother, I am proud to be your daughter. You gave me my humanity, you taught me the value of humility and solidarity, the love of work. Don't fear those who might harm you; be alert, keep your morale high, hold on to your dignity until death. That is the greatest legacy you can leave us.

There are so many things that I would have liked to have shared with you, but my life and thoughts belonged to my people from the time I was born. I carry with me your prayers, your sleepless nights – like those of so many mothers across the world.

You have always wanted the best of everything for me, my well-being. And what is my well-being? It is the hope that some day there will be real social justice in this country.

I love you,

Marta
National Police Headquarters
May 9, 1985.

The International Red Cross brought my mother and uncle Manuel to see me a week later. It had been so long since I had seen them! Even though my mother was carefully dressed, her suffering was evident in her face. Her eyes seemed smaller, her face was emaciated. I had to be strong. We both did. Our embrace seemed to last forever.

"I sacrificed so much for you, for your welfare," she said tearfully, "and look at you now! You're wounded, you're a prisoner! If only I could do something!"

"Yes, I know. You've given me so much. You have done everything humanly possible. Be at peace. It's you who taught me so many things about life...But I, too, did what I had to do; I'm doing what I must. I feel at peace."

I looked at her and felt our deep love and friendship once again. We were always very close. She looked to me for support. She respected my views, and consulted me about many things, including those which affected the family. I knew that she had been ill and was tremendously worried about me. That was why I had agreed that she should come and see me. Now we shared the pain and the infinite hope that one day we would be together again under better circumstances. She touched my wounds and caressed my hair. What courage! It was too painful to speak. The war had forced us to grow beyond our years.

I could not forget that the delegates from the International Red Cross were there, and I felt the cold stare of the detective. I did not want to let my suffering show in front of them.

I remembered all those times when I was a child and had not gotten my way, how I would pack my suitcases and threaten to run away from home. Or, other times, when I went away with the sisters for Holy Week or went on Christian retreats, how she always trusted me. Then later, when she realized I was not doing well in my classes at the university and that I was involved in the struggle, how angry she had been! We had argued and she had thrown me out of the house. She was so annoyed by our fight that she became ill, and a doctor had to be called. I was supposed to leave that day to do some work in a rural area. My sisters threatened to kill me if my mother died. The doctor told me I must apologize to her and undo the harm I had done. I told him he didn't know what was going on. I was torn, I felt something wrenching inside me. I had to decide whether to apologize for my participation in the struggle, or to swallow my pain and go on. I opted for the latter and moved to my older sister's house.

We were to have the same argument many times, until my

mother finally understood and accepted that I would not change my ideas. She had dreamed I would be a doctor and that I would marry a man who would make me happy, who would give me a stable social position. I'm not really sure what she thought when she suspected I had joined the guerrillas. Perhaps she just pretended she knew nothing. But we no longer fought over this. She began to express nationalist sentiments and I noticed a change in her attitude. I hid what I was doing from her anyway, telling her I was in graduate school in Mexico together with my husband.

She had always fussed over me. She worried about my appearance, about my health, even when we weren't near each other. It seemed she would never abandon her protective role. Sometimes this irritated me, as it clashed with my own independent nature. But I admired her warmth, her human quality. She was extremely patient and optimistic. When she saw I was worrying about something, she would enquire softly as to what was wrong. "Can I help you? Don't worry, everything will turn out fine. Look at things calmly, look at them from a positive perspective," she would say.

I hardly ever went to funerals, but once I went with her. While they were shovelling dirt on the coffin I was watching her and every so often she would turn to look at me. My eyes welled with tears. "Why are you crying?" she asked me in a low voice. "I didn't think you cared very much for Doña Emma."

"No, I'm not crying for her, but for you. I'm afraid of losing you, and not being able to be close to you again," I replied. She had always been such a source of moral support for me.

My uncle suggested we pray; he had brought a bible. He was a Baptist minister for a middle-class congregation. He began to pray. There were tears in his eyes as he looked at me. He had first found out about my revolutionary activity when he read the reports and saw the photos of the negotiations at La Palma. He said it was a real surprise and everyone had asked how could it be possible? "We never noticed anything 'abnormal'," my relatives remarked.

How did I see my family? They were hard-working people, but not directly exploited. They were the people who had filled my emotional life for many years. I used to get along better with some of mother's relatives than my father's family. Traditionally, I would take them to the cemetery on November 2, the day of the dead, to buy flowers for our grandparents' grave. On their birthdays I always did something, even if it was only calling to congratulate them on the phone.

My uncle, in many ways, had been like a father towards me. Now, once again, he was there in a difficult moment. He told me that he had been invited to give a poetry reading in the National Police Headquarters, despite his well-known anti-government views. The invitation was made by the chief of the political police, while I was still in the interrogation stage. A coincidence? Did they want me to know that they knew who my relatives were in order to pressure me?

My uncle was also watched since, after my mother left for Sweden, he was the one responsible for sending me clean clothing and sweets and monitoring my state of health. The packages were sent every eight days through the International Red Cross. Then the threats began. An explosive device was placed in a trash can in front of his house. He left for Sweden in September with my aunt María Elena and my older sister and her three children.

That day my mother told me that when I had appeared on television at La Palma, my son recognized me and shouted, "Look! There's my mommy!" "We told him it wasn't you but he insisted it was and grabbed the telephone; he wanted to call the helicopters so they would take him to you because he wanted to be with his mother," she said.

• Chapter 23 •

Tomorrow would mark one month since my capture. I felt life was eluding me. I was not brought into the world for this, I thought. I must resist in whatever way possible. I must learn to fight from within this cell. This will be my trench. But alone? Yes, if necessary. My life is the struggle for freedom. If I abandon that struggle, I will die of shame, especially knowing that the battle still raged outside.

Despite this pledge to myself, I still felt very heavy hearted. I wanted to demonstrate my resistance by supporting the hunger strike of other political prisoners demanding information about a disappeared prisoner, Janeth Samour. Despite the campaign, Janeth's whereabouts were still unknown. The regime had denied holding her. So, in spite of my weak physical condition, I decided to conduct a partial fast and not to eat from six in the evening until noon. In this manner I could show my solidarity with the striking *compas*.

The police became furious when I refused to eat. My food noticeably improved; it was not the same given to the rest of the prisoners. That day I sent a letter to the police chiefs in which I suggested that the improvement in my food was designed to improve their image:

National Police Headquarters   May 18, 1985

Chiefs, National Police

1) The improvement in my food comes along with other restrictive measures, such as the denial of access to fresh air or sun for even five minutes a day.

2) Despite the need for me to recuperate as soon as possible, in order to show my solidarity with my fellow women political prisoners struggling (already in their twenty-third day of a hunger strike) in order to present their just claims before the minister of justice and the Legislative Assembly, neither of which has agreed to listen to them;

3) Being aware of my condition, my specific situation and responsibility for my own actions,

I have resolved:

That beginning on May 18 to engage in a "partial fast," that is, to not eat between 6 p.m. and 12 p.m. in solidarity with the women political prisoners until they end their hunger strike.

My life is the struggle for freedom; if I abandon that struggle, I will die of shame...

Commander Nidia Díaz

I was intransigent. I accepted the special food because I had to regain my strength in order to hasten my recovery and be in good shape. This was the only way I could continue to resist. Meanwhile, I was being denied my rights, such as time outside in the sun.

Colonel Revelo, director of the National Police, passed by that night. "Nidia," he said, "it would be better for you to show solidarity with yourself and your son. You're very weak and have to get better. You shouldn't stop eating or you'll make yourself sick."

"It doesn't matter. I feel strong and don't need a lot of food. I should go on a total hunger strike."

Days later, to my surprise, they opened my cell and told me, "Nidia, you're going out." At this point, my foot was in a cast and I still had a splint on my right arm. I held the crutch under my left arm.

"I'm going out?"

"We'll help you," said the detective, who had arrived with two others.

"Where am I going?"

"To get some sun," said one.

"To get some sun?"

"Yes, of course. Why not?" he said.

The sun felt so good, yet different from what I remembered of that April 18, the day of my capture. Then it was so brilliant, so overwhelming. Now, the sky was an intense blue and it seemed I had never before fully appreciated the beauty of the sun and the sky.

But the two storey police headquarters cast a shadow over the yard, and a number of police and agents were on the balconies, filling the terraces, watching me. I was angry, but kept my face raised towards the sun. Life flowed back into me in those ten minutes. It was as if the sun's rays penetrated the very depths of my being.

Part Four

Fears,
hopes
and
memories

Of the terrible pain
(July 5, 1985)

Through these thirty-two bars
facing a wall
I feel a bitter-sweet nostalgia
memories of times past
that fill me with love –
I neither weep, nor grieve.

I feel a yearning filled with faith,
faith in the future.
I do not seek it out
but it finds me here.

The present brings terrible pain
and simple joy,
I cry and I sing.

I feel within me the rebellion,
the resistance of the ages,
within my people
within our struggle.

All joined in one voice
the song of humanity.
The past,
the present,
the future.

• Chapter 24 •

I felt a desperate urge to run, but couldn't even walk because of the cast that had recently been put on my leg. I couldn't stand being like this. Dr. Bottari and others told me I had appeared on television. I kept asking myself: What do they want? What is going on? Surely there is nothing I have said they could use against the struggle. What disturbed me the most was when they said Castellanos and two others had appeared on the same program.

Lieutenant Serpas, chief of the National Police political section, came to question me. He told me video clips were shown in which I admitted that documents had been found on me and that I was affected by Miguel Castellanos's treason. So that was how they planned to simply undermine the confidence of the people! I also learnt they reported that the Armed Forces were obstructing the operation on my arm and that I ran the risk of complications. This possibility apparently caused some alarm.

I heard for myself the Armed Forces' press office say on radio that a large number of documents were found on me. It suited them to mention this now I had been imprisoned over a month. They hoped the television clip would improve their credibility. They would manipulate anything for their own purposes. The number of papers found on me was grossly exaggerated and to my disgust they even attributed some CIA documents to me.

Only now, after a month, Duarte publicly referred to the documents that had been found on me and claimed I was responsible for leading a strike. I began to realize that, considering the efforts they were making, things couldn't be going well for the government. The big delay, the unbelievable number of documents they said I had in my backpack and the obvious fabrication of their contents – these weren't factors that helped the regime's credibility with the media. The exaggeration, the hype were too blatant. Nevertheless, I feared for our movement.

May was the most difficult month. It was now almost the 31st. My situation wasn't easy to bear: the regime was manipulating information, my family was under the terror of constant threats and attacks, and they had used my appearance on video tapes without my knowing how I was being presented. I felt I was between four walls facing a bigger wall.

I withstood the daily visits by Dr. Bottari. He came to see if I was holding up to the pressure of endless interrogations in the adjoining cell. I also saw the other prisoners go past blindfolded. I felt the watchful glances of the detectives, laying in wait, twenty-four hours a day. But I uttered not one complaint, nor admitted that I was about to go mad, or pleaded for a tranquilizer. I convinced myself to keep up the struggle, if only with pen and paper. I wrote a letter to Revelo demanding a press conference. I had the right to defend myself, to leave my record of the facts. I had the right to denounce before the world that my family was being persecuted.

National Police Headquarters
May 27, 1985

Colonel Revelo (N.P. Director):
I am writing to request that you allow me to hold a press conference for the national and international press here in the National Police Headquarters.

I am greatly angered and consider the essential reasons for this conference are:

1) To clarify the distortions and misuse of the documents that were confiscated at the time of my capture. This propaganda game is being carried out specifically by the Salvadoran Armed Forces High Command and the U.S. Embassy. General Blandon is deceptively attributing to me documents found at perhaps another time and place, or that have been fabricated with information given by the traitor Miguel Castellanos. An example of such documents are those that refer to contradictions between the FDR and the FMLN; the contradictions between the Sandinistas in Nicaragua and the FMLN, the Nicaraguan government commitment, or FMLN commitments to fight in Nicaragua if the U.S. invades that country.

Another example is the documents that compromise

the June 21 Andes agreement by stating that the FMLN has been preparing and training abroad (in Communist countries) since 1970.

2) These documents were not in my backpack and this can be proven by the fact that they do not have bullet holes through them like the rest of my papers.

The Armed Forces High Command is displaying the greatest opportunism and cynicism with a prisoner of war, and has the complicity of the Christian Democratic government. A great farce is being performed by the U.S. Embassy and the Armed Forces' press office in its psychological war against the people.

3) I denounce the Salvadoran Armed Forces High Command, specifically Blandon and the chiefs of staff. I also denounce the intelligence department of the political police since they are the ones who have investigated me, and for the threats and attacks inflicted on my family. I hold those named above responsible from this moment on for any harm that comes to my mother, my son, or any family member. I accuse them of not yet having rid the Salvadoran Armed Forces of those elements that are, in one way or another, to a greater or lesser degree, backed by and connected to the so-called death squads.

I am also informing you that I am in the eleventh day of a "partial fast" in solidarity with the women political prisoners who are on a hunger strike in order to have their just claims heard, as well as to protest the government's failure to verify the whereabouts of Commander Janet Samour and *compañera* Maximina.

I extend my thanks to you for having called Legal Aid on May 26 at my request.

My life is the struggle for freedom; if I abandon that struggle, I will die of shame.

Commander Nidia Díaz

When, three days later, I still had not received a reply from Revelo I wrote him another letter, accusing him of complicity in everything that was happening to me.

National Police Headquarters
May 30, 1985

Colonel Revelo:

Last night, you came by my cell and I asked you
whether you had received my letter (dated May 27). You
said you had.

By the very fact that I am writing, you may think I am
"politically naive" or that "I don't understand politics."
But you must understand that I am doing so in order to
leave an historical record; I wish to defend myself from
the abuse and lack of respect to which, as a political
person (although I am a prisoner), you subject me. Yes,
all of you because you Colonel, are indisputably part of
the Salvadoran Armed Forces and in agreement with the
High Command and chiefs of staff and, of course, with the
policy of President Duarte.

However, I want you to know that I will not rest until
the day I can clarify everything. Sooner or later, the truth
will be known. You know that everything changes and I,
one way or another, even DEAD, will have the
opportunity...

A few days later, Revelo came by and told me he could not
allow me to hold the press conference I had requested. Meanwhile
the humanitarian organizations informed me that they were
continuing to harass my mother and were looking for my son.

I was overcome with sadness the day the International Red
Cross representatives entered my cell. They asked why I was
crying. I quickly dried my tears and began to explain how
important it was for me to give my side of the story to the press.
"In a press conference," I explained, "I would be able to let the
world know that my family is being harassed and that it is
completely untrue I was carrying so many documents. Why don't
they say that they were bombing civilians that day?"

"There are a lot of journalists who want to talk with you. But
the Military High Command won't let them. They've tried using
every means possible but permission has been refused."

"Of course," I said. "They allow them to come only when it

suits their purposes."

Once again, I awoke with the desperate sensation of wanting to escape. How much longer would I be there? As long as is necessary, Nidia, I told myself. They had decided to take their revenge by keeping me there, right next to the interrogation cell. I couldn't stand it. Of course, one prepares oneself to resist and to suffer. And we are people who will fight for our rights until the last breath. So much blood has not flowed for nothing. The political prisoners' hunger strike was not in vain. I had to stand beside them in solidarity. But I shouldn't have been there any more. I had to insist on my transfer.

I sang a lot during those days, almost all the time. I sang for myself and the other prisoners. I don't have a good voice, but I sang anyway. I had to let my feelings out.

> My people, give me your happiness
> I swear they shall not conquer me.
> My people, give me your courage
> I swear to return it to you.
> My friends have all gone,
> others shall come after them.
> I am sorry, because I loved
> their sweet company.
> What shall be with my life?
> I do not know.
> If I have done much, if I have done little
> Tomorrow we shall know
> Tomorrow we shall see
> And what shall be, shall be.

I had to survive between those four walls. I looked around. There was a table, a chair and a desk. I had pencils and pens and later I had watercolors which the regime allowed the solidarity movement to send. I arranged everything like a small desk. I cut out some pictures of people and landscapes from a magazine and pasted them on the wall.

I already had a radio. I had actually been sent two but I gave one to the other political prisoners. It was hard to get anything, but I was supported by the Red Cross and Legal Aid. These were rights that had been won by the political prisoners' organization. It was incredible but the degree of the people's combativeness, maturity and level of organization could be felt – even in prison.

Several officers passed by and said, "You're pretty comfortable there, aren't you? You can't complain about anything."

"All I need are some plants," I said.

"You want plants?"

"Yes. I asked the Human Rights Commission for a flowering plant but it wasn't permitted."

"We'll send you one tomorrow," Revelo promised.

I love nature. Even to see a single leaf would have been enough. There was nothing green at Police Headquarters; everything was cement – cement walls and cement floors. I yearned for a plant.

• Chapter 25 •

Very early the next morning, they brought in a large planter. One of the officers cynically remarked that it had been prepared just for me. It had been found stuffed with weapons in Santa Ana. It was large and rectangular and had only one plant with just one leaf left on it. It was the most ironic thing they could have done – a half-dead plant. I told them to take it away, but they ignored me.

Time passed more quickly now. I organized my survival so that I kept busy almost all day and I made sure everything I did helped my state of mind. At 5 a.m. they came in to clean my cell – the International Red Cross insisted on proper cleanliness because of my physical condition. My family had sent disinfectant. I would get up and exercise as much as I could for about forty-five minutes. I had a cast on an arm and another on my leg, so I did not have great freedom of movement. I listened to the news, the volume turned down. Then I would bathe and get dressed. I washed my underwear with my left hand. It was complicated for me to bathe since I had to put plastic bags on my leg and arm with my good hand. Because of the lice, I needed to wash my hair every day as well. They refused to believe I had lice but one of the nurses promised to give me some anti-lice soap. After I went out to get some sun I would come back inside to read or write. It was very difficult to write since I couldn't hold a pen very well. I began to draw. Somehow, I passed the time. Most importantly, I managed to communicate with the other prisoners – using hand signals in between the bars – without the detective realizing what I was doing.

It became easier to bear the continuous racket next door – the sound of the interrogations, the slamming of the door to Cell 21, the incessant noise of the construction machinery – when I was busy. I found I could extract myself from what was going on.

At night I had the picture of the ballerina to look at; she kept urging me to walk, reminding me how I used to dance and could do so again. Next to her the woman on horseback rode through the countryside, pointing the way that I would follow again one day.

The first time I traveled to the countryside on a political assignment was the summer of 1974 in Suchitoto. I had to walk alone for about six kilometers and every step of the way seemed to reaffirm my resolve. I arrived at the contact point, a cross-roads, where I met two *compañeros* who led me to an adobe house. There was a hammock hanging from the ceiling beams.

I remember asking Manuel, a farm worker, why he wanted to join the guerrillas. He told me how he and his family had worked as live-in laborers on a large farm. He smiled a wide toothless smile as he described how one of the big watch-dogs on this farm had a gold tooth, while he had none. He bitterly resented this, especially as he had to feed meat to these dogs while he and his family went without. Occasionally they would steal the meat, but the farmer would be furious if he found some of Manuel's six children eating any. Manuel died in combat in 1980.

After this experience I would always ask the same question on arriving at a new place.

I knew the time would come when we would no longer have to use buses to get around; when we would have established "corridors" to move through and travel with greater freedom, something we have now accomplished. By 1976 it was easier, especially under the cover of night. I would sleep in the ditches and walk all over the hills and valleys. My feet yearned to walk there again.

I was constantly tortured by thoughts of my mistakes. What were the *compañeros* thinking of me, of the stand I had taken? Perhaps I had made errors other than those of the day I was captured. I asked myself over and over: Did they think I had betrayed them? Little did I realize that I had in fact become an inspiration to my *compañeros*, that they suffered for me, and had even composed songs and poems for me.

> I saw you on TV yesterday, Nidia,
> with plaster on your arm and leg,
> the enemy announced
> they had you prisoner,
> someone next to me said:
> "she's a lioness."

> We know that your heart
> has not been imprisoned,
> that there is no plaster, hood,
> electric shocks that can bind it.
> There, before the cameras
> and in the torture chamber
> you have been our banner and our hope
> a strong bastion, a silent soldier.

> With such simplicity
> you have mocked
> their strategy of death
> their shamelessness.

and:

> Wounded by their murderous fire
> they wanted to use her
> in their machiavellian game.
> They locked her up
> in their sanctuary of death
> using their subtle and vile tortures
> but could not unclench her fist...

rather, her love moved
and made the tyrant tremble
in his hiding place...

There were also the words written by an anonymous woman in a book sent to me. She said she was one of the many thousands of women who struggled for peace and tried to follow my example. She told me to go forward – that their hopes were with me.

On one occasion one of the members of the government's Human Rights Commission kissed me as he was leaving, catching me off-guard. I just stood there staring at him, and he kissed me again. "Forgive me *compañera*, I had to do that in the name of the people. Please don't say anything," he said.

Who was I to them? How did they see me? I didn't know, but I didn't believe I was anyone special. I felt I was simply carrying out my responsibility. I was disconcerted by the many things projected on to me by people. A few days before, I had received some scribblings that said everyone there was aware of my situation, that they loved me. They told me to be strong, that we should develop mutual trust and protect each other.

Some of those detained in Cell 16 were evangelists; I had nicknamed them "The Singers" because they sang all day long. They were peasants from the east and had been arbitrarily arrested by troops from the Fourth Military Detachment in Morazán. Since their arrest, no one had been able to prove anything against them. They had been savagely beaten over the period of a week; now they had spent two weeks undergoing interrogation. They were continually accused of collaborating with the FMLN. They regularly sang for me, dedicating the "Psalm of the Hundred Sheep" to me:

...Christ, you have seen her suffer
help her, don't let her falter...

• Chapter 26 •

Following the instructions of the doctors from the Red Cross, staff from the Military Hospital came one afternoon to do an electromyogram so that the extent of the damage to my right arm could be determined. Getting approval to conduct the test had entailed a long process; even the Military High Command had to be consulted first. It was a test that should have been conducted at the hospital, but they did it in the registration room at the jail. There were many problems because of electrical interference.

The machine had needles and prongs and electrical wires; it looked like it would be a painful experience. It seemed everyone around me agreed with this appreciation of the situation. They had all come to watch the spectacle: the interrogators, the detectives. Every time a shock was applied they watched me closely, but my pride was stronger than the pain – I did not flinch. Noticing that I had not complained, one of them remarked, "You've got guts, Nidia."

I felt strangely detached from what was happening. I was thinking about the recent news reports I had heard. At dawn a few days earlier, the office of the non-government Human Rights Commission had been broken into – money had been taken and secret documentation of cases stolen. That same day there had been another demonstration by striking national waterworks workers. Fifty workers had already been fired. The Nineteenth Congress of ANDES (National Association of Salvadoran Teachers) was drawing to a close with delegations from the United States in attendance. There was no doubt that the struggle was advancing. Suddenly, I felt the needles again.

That night, two officers in camouflage uniform passed by my cell. There was something odd about them; they stopped and watched me. The detective went up to them. "Is that Nidia?" they asked.

"Yes," he answered. "That's her."

They looked me over intently and then left. Soon after, the

watch officer came along, asking which way they had gone. "No one is allowed to come this way. Don't ever let anyone see her again," he ordered.

I shuddered. I realized that those two men had been casing the place and that any day someone could come by and kill me in the same casual manner. Others had come before them and certainly others would come in the future.

My spirits were higher by that time. The struggle of my people was intensifying. After almost three years of lull, the popular movement was on the rise again. The mass movement was ever more creative. During 1980 and 1981 the Christian Democratic junta had dealt tremendous blows against the working class organizations, practically eradicating their leadership. Now they were appearing again with renewed energy, under a new and expanding generation of mass leaders.

It was dark when about ten people were brought out of the interrogation cell. I was standing by the bars. One of them looked directly at me and smiled when his blindfold was removed; he looked pleased to see me. I didn't remember ever having seen him before, but I liked him. I smiled back. I would find out later they were all union leaders who were regularly dragged in and out of interrogation sessions. After that, whenever they came by, or when I knew they were being interrogated, I would sing for them:

> The Salvadoran people
> have the sky for a hat,
> so tall has grown their dignity
> throughout their search
> for a flowering of the earth,
> for the cleansing joy
> that will spring
> from those who have fallen.
>
> Press on, Salvadorans, press on
> there is no small bird
> that would stop in mid-air
> once he has started to fly.
> Press on, Salvadorans, press on.

Among those imprisoned trade unionists were the secretary general and the negotiations secretary of the Social Security Union who had been arrested during a strike for better wages. A violent helicopter raid had been launched on the Central Social Security Hospital early in June.

The raid operation had been directed by Reinaldo López Nuila, vice-minister for public security. They employed Treasury Police troops as the landing force, with masks and dressed in black, reinforced by the National Police, who had earlier infiltrated cops into the strike. The troops were so nervous that the Treasury Police managed to kill four of the undercover National Police – in spite of the fact that within the first few minutes they already had everyone tied up and lying face down on the ground. The police arrested all the strike leaders. In open challenge, the workers announced they would continue their strike until their leaders were freed. The same happened months later during the strike of the Popular Credit Bank workers, when their secretary general was arrested.

Neither arrests nor disappearances, assassinations of union leaders, nor searches of their locals or military raids could break the will of the workers. Article 29 of the political constitution and the Decree 296, which were meant to impede the mobilization of workers and deny the right to strike, had proved equally ineffective.

One of the trade unionists who passed by me looked a little like my brother, only he was not intellectually disabled like my dear Rafael.

I first became involved in organizing workers in the 1970's. Every time I remember that stage of the struggle, I think of the poems written by Commander Susana:

> Long live the working class
> the leaders of the poor
> and long live the peasants
> their most steady and loyal ally...
>
> If you could only understand
> this pain of separation,
> this growing pain that makes me live

and makes me survive.
If you of so few and tender years
could see this pain,
you would move the world,
you would shatter the universe
of the unknown.

My son had been born five weeks premature. Our work at the time was very demanding and our responsibilities increased every day. We were living through a period of resistance, trying to consolidate our forces in order to advance. I was working in the urban front, working clandestinely under a false identity. I had over-stretched myself and at times had to walk very long distances. I had almost miscarried earlier.

I remember the indescribable joy I felt when I gave birth and I saw my little one. From deep inside I felt such a new and intense tenderness. This, I thought, was one more responsibility, but one of a different nature: the responsibility to give life. I had planted a seed. He looked exactly like his father. For the next few days I kept putting a pillow over my belly; it felt strange without him inside of me, rather cold.

Dear one, my gorgeous one,
don't ever forget me.
I am somewhere between
heaven and hell.
I am a mortal that has
somehow been made immortal.

I have survived, I'm alive,
don't ever forget me.
I don't know when I'll see you,
perhaps soon,
perhaps not.
One can never know the surprises life holds.
I am here now, doing what I must.

The first time I was separated from him he was six months old and I was still nursing him. It was dawn. My mother gave me her blessing and said, "Don't worry, go ahead. My love for him is double: this child is the fruit of your womb and you're the fruit of mine. How could I not do everything to care for and protect him!"

We were both crying. When I left, I felt as if I was being torn inside. Each time I had to leave him I fretted I would never see him again; I feared he would no longer recognize me, that he would reject me. That first time, it was two months before I saw him again. Initially he hesitated. After that it was fine.

He had to have two hernia operations when he was two months old. Then, at four months, he had to have a cast on one leg because of a birth defect on one of his feet. I used to worry excessively about him; I think I tended to over-protect him. Whenever I was with him I would check every inch of his body very carefully.

Remember, little Alejandro
that we still have to play,
to talk,
to share our tenderness.

Wait for me with open arms
whether here or in heaven
or in the immortal history
of this our people.

• Chapter 27 •

June 19 was the day my mother, my son, my sister and her daughter were forced into exile from their homeland. What could they expect to find in Sweden, thousands of kilometers away? I was sure it would be very hard for them to feel at home in that society.

My anxiety for them grew, and turned to anguish when I found out that the political police had been making threats against my mother and had even dared to riddle her house with machine-gun fire. The bullets had missed her head by only ten centimeters. They had followed her; hooded men had arrived at the house looking for her. There were constant phone calls asking about my son, threatening to kidnap him. They would tell my mother that she only had hours left to live or that they were placing a bomb in her house. She was told to leave the country or she would be killed. All this was intended to make me feel guilty and responsible.

The threats had started after my mother came to see me at the jail together with the International Red Cross. One lieutenant had the gall to tell me that my mother was being persecuted by the guerrillas, who were out to avenge my supposed betrayal.

My mother, feeling seriously threatened, had sought help from the archbishop's office and the International Committee for Migrants. That was how she had made the arrangements to go to Sweden, a country which offers refuge to the victims of war. There are thousands of Salvadoran refugees in Sweden, as well as Australia, Canada, Honduras, Costa Rica, Nicaragua, and Mexico.

In her desperation, my mother even wrote to Duarte describing the persecution she was suffering. Duarte answered that he would conduct the necessary investigations. Of course he did nothing.

In El Salvador the relatives of guerrilla fighters – especially relatives of the movement leaders – usually become victims themselves of persecution. They may be killed or disappeared as a form of pressure and to teach us a lesson. When they find we can't be broken, the regime attacks those who are left defenseless. If we're in jail, they try to increase the pressure on us by arresting our relatives; it's an effort at blackmail to try and break your will. They'll play tapes of their voices. If you have a small child, they'll play the voice of a crying child. When Graciela was prisoner they arrested her father and undressed her in his presence. They assassinated Ana Guadalupe's brother, and they bombed Commander Villalobos's father's shop and took him prisoner.

This they do for vengeance alone. In my case twelve[1] of my relatives became victims of the repression and were forced into

1. My brother-in-law had been kidnapped and had been held and tortured by the Treasury Police during seventeen days. Because of the pressure applied in his case, the government of El Salvador released him to the Swedish government.

exile. They had nothing to do with the FMLN; their crime was solely to be related to me, and to have regularly sent me clean clothes.

As I thought of my family leaving for exile, and the plight of so many other families, I could hold back the tears no longer. Face down on my bed I imagined the face of my child, such a gentle face. I felt his olive skin. There was always sadness in his exquisitely sensitive eyes. He was born the year of "the offensive" (1981). I remembered his father and how it was not easy to decide to have a child in the midst of a war, much less with the kinds of responsibilities we had at the time. The wish is always there to have a child — even many — who'll be born and develop in the struggle, to carry on after us, to watch them grow alongside the process. There will never be enough time to enjoy them, but you know they're there. It's not easy to think that you will be separated from them for indefinite periods of time; that they might have to grow up as orphans. Worse yet, that they might become one of the disappeared, or perhaps assassinated before your own eyes. Captured children are usually taken to correctional centers. Osmín had been taken there until some nuns rescued him.

You know in your heart that your son is part of your people and that, even if they harm him in order to hurt and intimidate you, you will never betray or deliver anyone to them. That is precisely why it's so difficult. You want to watch your children grow, you want to enjoy them and that's not always possible in times of war. You must live intensely every moment you have with them, share with them all you have learnt in order to make them better than you are. The light of the future is in their small hands.

> My small son
> my little big man
> I don't know when I'll see you again.
> But one day
> I will see you,
> and once again my love
> and gentleness for you
> will overflow
> and I will be your friend once again.

I could see Osmín as he stood there with Chabelita and six others. He wasn't very tall, and only nine years old – one of thousands of other children. His back was bleeding; his courage filled me with admiration and taught me so much. Osmín did not play in the bright sunshine like my José Alejandro did – like I wish all the children of my country could play. This is why I struggle. Did my little big man understand?

I was certain that I would see my son again; I just couldn't imagine when or where.

• Chapter 28 •

I was sketching a landscape, one of those hills over which my feet have often walked, when a group of officers and North Americans stopped in front of my cell. They opened the cell door and five of them came in. They were congressmen, they said. They explained to me that people in the United States were interested in my health and wanted to know how I was doing. I told them that I had been demanding a transfer to the women's prison; that I was being held unfairly and arbitrarily at Police Headquarters, which was not in accordance with established laws. I explained why I wanted to be transferred, and I informed them of the threats and persecution which my family had suffered.

They appeared not to listen to what I was saying. It was apparent that the real motive for their visit was something else. "What is your opinion of the massacre in the Zona Rosa?" they asked.

"It came about because of U.S. intervention in our country. Your direct participation in the war exposes you to such danger. You are involved more and more every day but you do not want to accept the risks, which is impossible. I was captured by a Yankee. Duarte hasn't been able to deny it. You're now involved in the actual war zones. Perhaps an invasion will be the next step."

"Nidia, is there a connection between your capture and the case of the Zona Rosa? Did the PRTC carry out a massacre because it was a North American who captured you?"

"What happened to me is only an infinitesimal part of your intervention. For over six years increasing U.S. involvement has delayed the resolution of the conflict. It's your bombs that are dropped on us. It is you who train the battalions that carry out terrorist acts. The tactics of the war are determined by the Pentagon and its advisers. They are the tactics of terror."

"Was it an act of desperation?"

"I don't know who you are or what you're looking for, but I will tell you that El Salvador is filled with dozens of advisers, expert torturers, CIA agents and U.S. officials. They are linked to the disappearances, the torture, the arrests, and the interrogations. It is they who direct and control the intelligence services."

"But it was only innocent people who died there."

"Look," I replied, "our enemy is imperialism, not the Salvadoran people. The FMLN is tired of fighting soldiers who have been recruited by force while their officers and the North Americans can stroll down the street enjoying themselves. From now on, we're going after those who are responsible."

"How do you see your support in the United States? You might have had their sympathy before. After this massacre, you're going to lose it."

"I'm sure that the people of the United States will understand. In this case, even though it was an action by the PRTC, it was in keeping with the line of the General Command of the FMLN and not an act of terrorism. It was a legitimate defensive action against those who foster and organize the aggression against Nicaragua and El Salvador, against those who support the contras and the Duarte government."

"Admit you made a mistake – innocent people were hurt."

"I'm not familiar with the details. But we do not take any actions unless we have specific information. I'm sure they were advisers or CIA agents."

They looked at each other and then left hurriedly. Was this an interrogation? I don't think so, they didn't appear to be policemen. Besides, they said they were congressmen – that's what the interpreter said. Funny, Revelo and the officers he was with were in civilian clothes.

The night they were referring to had been a terrible night for me. The *Mardoqueo Cruz* commandos had undertaken an opera-

116

tion named "Yankee aggressors: another Vietnam awaits you in El Salvador." They attacked some U.S. advisers and intelligence agents who were dining at a restaurant in the Zona Rosa, in San Salvador. That night my entire body shook with trepidation and my heart pounded; I smoked a whole pack of cigarettes. I feared I would be dragged out again for interrogation, or that they would take me out and have me kidnapped while being transferred to the women's jail. I speculated on a thousand possibilities. Two days went by with no one claiming responsibility for the Zona Rosa action. I had time to assess the situation.

The action had been successful. It was part of a period of actions that demonstrated a qualitative change in the effectiveness of the FMLN in the main urban centers. It was the result of the experience and the effort of our commandos in San Salvador. The backbone of the operation was the broad support from different sectors of the population. Without that support it would have been impossible to carry out.

The military situation in the zone was not advantageous. The headquarters of the chiefs of staff of the Armed Forces and the military academy were only about 250 meters away. The barracks of the San Benito battalion of the National Police were close by. The Brazilian embassy was ten meters across the street. In addition, the minister of defense, the U.S. ambassador and many members of the oligarchy lived nearby; these included Jorge Bustamante, the director of social security, who refused to negotiate with the workers during a strike. All of their residences were protected by permanent security forces.

According to the news, the *compañeros* had also machine-gunned the chief of staff's installations and Bustamante's residence. For such an action, it was necessary to organize research, identification and review teams. It had required the organized support of activists, supporters, and sympathizers, all of them coordinated through a communications network under the direct orders of the rebel military command.

Three commandos had participated in the action: one with the task of confrontation and elimination, and one each for immediate and medium term security. They all had to be adequately armed. The *compañeros* arrived at the Zona Rosa and surveyed the area: the restaurant, the U.S. advisers and CIA agents. When the shooting started civilian security forces in the area responded, creating a cross-fire.

The commandos had a time frame of a maximum of four minutes to complete the action and withdraw. By the time the military surrounded the area and troops entered the scene the *compañeros* were out of danger. Julio Martínez had died heroically during this action.

That day, June 19, hell was raised at the National Police Headquarters. They were enraged. One could hear news broadcasts being played continuously. I was very happy, but could not speak out as I wanted to, to let my prison comrades and those undergoing interrogation know what had happened. Several officers came by, including Revelo, López Dávila, and Serpas. "Good evening, Nidia," said Revelo, putting his hand to his forehead as always.

I began to sweat. I swallowed the smoke I had in my mouth, raised my head and looked straight at him. "Good evening," I responded.

Silence. Everyone was looking at me. They kept watching me. I had to take advantage of the situation and be the first one to speak. "What's happening with my transfer to Ilopango? I have written and appealed and have not received an answer."

"Your case is being reviewed by the military judge. María Julia called and said she would come next week with a judicial expert. Also, Monsignor Rivera is supposed to come see you. If you want to see the Engineer, he will come."

"The engineer? What engineer?"

"Engineer Duarte. He has told me that if you wish, he will come and see you."

I couldn't believe it, but I did not let on. I tried to ignore the question but he pressed for an answer. "Not like this, not from behind bars. Never!" I answered.

I turned to address Revelo in a very calm voice, all the while looking López Dávila in the eye. "I want to tell you that about two days ago an interrogator came by with some pictures of a woman. Not even anyone I know. I consider that a form of interrogation, and I will let the International Red Cross and Legal Aid know about it. I don't want it to happen again. My interrogation period is over. That's an abuse."

Revelo looked to López Dávila and then looked at me. "Don't be concerned, Nidia; they won't come to bother you again," he said.

I could not sleep all night; I smoked too much. I've never really had a cigarette habit, much less an obsessive one. Even during interrogation I had refused to accept the cigarettes they frequently offered me. Dawn finally arrived.

The news report said that a military operation over Morazán had been completed. Heroic Morazán! If I could have just listened – even for only a minute – to either Radio Venceremos or the Farabundo Martí station, but I couldn't get it there with all the interference. Besides, the cop who was always in front of my cell would stop me. Morazán! How well I knew Morazán, its territory, its depths, the guerrillas, their commanders, the battles...I could feel my friends around me again.

That night I was on edge, wracked with worry. I thought about the war and about the political excuses the government invented to justify its aggression. I thought of the *compañeros*, the fighters. I felt like I'd let them down. Maybe they expected better of me. I wondered how those who were undergoing interrogation were doing. I kept hearing the ceaseless questions: "Isn't it true that this is the structure of your organization?...Do you recognize her?...And him?...And him?" "No, no, I don't know them..." Sometimes there was no answer at all.

I was a prisoner of war, that was my situation. What was the best thing for me to do? How should I conduct myself? I reminded myself I was only doing what I thought was right, but somehow I felt it was not enough. I missed all those places where my feet used to roam. Central America...the fields, mountains, cities. My loved ones. The reunions and the partings.

> Through these thirty-two bars
> facing a wall
> I feel a bitter-sweet nostalgia
> memories of times past
> that fill me with love –
> I neither weep, nor grieve.

• Chapter 29 •

For a week I had been very miserable. I wondered what was going on inside me. It was like a premonition of something terrible about to happen. I could not figure it out, until one morning when I went out to get some sun and Lieutenant Serpas came up to me and said mockingly: "Shit, babe! You have a great memory."

"Why do you say that?"

"The report you wrote and were able to send your party – you told them about each and every one of the papers you were carrying in your backpack, you even had them organized by subject in the report. And you told them step by step about all the stages of your interrogation."

What a shock! I froze from head to toe, filled with fear. Somehow I managed to look at him calmly and say, "What report? I've sent nothing out of here!"

All the while questions kept running over each other in my mind: How can they know about it? Have they captured the person who was smuggling it out? Why now, if it's been two months? When and how did they get their hands on that report?

"Don't play dumb with me, babe! You wrote a forty-two page report, twenty-one sheets on both sides; it was in your handwriting. You told them how inexperienced we were and how you had been able to win us over."

"You're lying! I haven't written anything," I answered firmly.

"Oh? So what was it that Arlen Siu was carrying in her backpack?"

I started to choke up.

"Arlen Siu who?"

"Arlen Siu. The commander killed in the north of San Miguel. Are you going to tell me now that you didn't know her? She copped it along with a lot of other terrorists. The Third Brigade wiped you all out."

Then everything became clear. They had increased the guards during the last week with two cops – one watching the other.

They had changed all the staff of the government's Human Rights Commission; they allowed only one representative of the Red Cross to see me, and he couldn't visit me alone; and, they had arrested one of the members of the Legal Aid staff. My right to receive the newspapers had been suspended without explanation.

"Look babe, I would have broken you if I hadn't felt sorry for you. God! you were so pitiful. We lost a lot of time in your case; we coddled you. We were interrupted all the time, taking you out for the press or the doctors to see you. It wasn't that we couldn't have broken you if we had really tried."

He was trying to provoke me. I smiled and said, "Well, I guess it's too bad that there are people such as yourself, who do not carry out their orders. It was your responsibility to break me, to soften me up to see if I would break. But let me ask you, don't you think it was more than enough to have interrogated me without letting me sleep a single night, a single moment? To harass me continually, without allowing me a single pain killer?"

"You must be joking! We didn't even interrogate you for fifteen days straight. Don't you remember we had to take you in and out: you had to have an X-ray, we let the Red Cross come to see you. I felt sorry for you – that's all. Don't you remember that I would come see you and not even question you?"

"I know your voice. I know you interrogated me. You need to rationalize your defeat; you cannot accept that there are people who live by their principles and who will die before they betray."

"No way – not if we really turn up the pressure. In your case I just didn't try. Look, I was the one who broke Miguel Castellanos. I used everything that I learnt in Chile, Uruguay, and Venezuela, only more creatively. No one can resist me. I just felt sorry for you, that's all."

"You're provoking me, you'd like an opportunity to start the interrogation again. If you say that you could have broken me and didn't, I guess you lost your opportunity. It's gone."

I almost spat at him. This rat always came up to me when I was getting some sun, trying to play the nice guy. In fact, he was the chief of the political police. In the beginning he had tried to hide who he was and acted like he was only one of the administrative staff. He kept telling me he had known me as a child, and always called me his *cipota* [little girl] in a mocking tone. He was one of the few officers who dared to disrespect me and continued to interrogate me unofficially, like he was doing that morning. Not even Major López Dávila, chief of intelligence, would have dared to question me in such a manner.

I had had enough. I turned my back and went upstairs hurriedly. He still shouted after me, in a mocking voice, "Hey, you're not mad at me, are you?"

Every time I recalled that incident I became more enraged. I couldn't stop thinking about Arlen. She was dead! The next morning in the early news of Radio YSU they announced that Commander Arlen Siu Guazapa had died in combat.

Arlen Siu, my comrade, my friend, my sister. Death had caught up with her this June. Through tears I stared at the picture of the woman on horseback and that day she looked like Arlen. Then I understood the sadness I had felt in the last few days; it was for her even though I didn't know it. The light from her eyes will light my darkness and her voice will be the morning bird of our dawning.

We met in 1973, when we had psychology classes together. We were to meet many times after that. And now, her spirit would become part of our effort in building a unified party. I hadn't seen her for four months. She had just been put in charge of the political-military work in the eastern region. I couldn't believe that she was no longer there, among us. She was always cheerful, always singing. She gave her soul to every organizing task and into every new recruit. Her warmth and solidarity were our protection in winter. She had so many projects, so much initiative. We will feel her presence in the afternoon combats, her tiny form will lead us at the head of each guerrilla column, as her courage fires from every weapon.

Her human spirit helped others to understand more clearly the tasks and the problems in the grassroots organizations. She had helped organize the children and the women in each of the different fronts. She had loved children so much – and finally she was going to be a mother! She was pregnant when they killed her; about to bring one more little fighter into the world. Her love will live in every free Salvadoran child; her blood has fed this land, preparing it for freedom. Her joy will be my companion, Arlen – Celia – *always onwards to victory!*

122

I became obsessed with thoughts of all the loved ones who were no longer with us. The death of Arlen Siu made me want to improve myself, to fill her shoes as I crossed those valleys, to pick up her gun and aim for both of us. She was a truly courageous woman, who had worked and excelled in all the war fronts, including prison, our fifth front.

Later, I learnt that she was killed on June 26, 1985, six days after the second anniversary of the death in combat of her companion, Mardoqueo Cruz. What a coincidence! They had been together in life and now were reunited through the legacy of their example. I had worked with Mardoqueo in the development of the urban fronts in 1982 and 1983. He came from a working class family. Now, the urban guerrillas carried his name and vindicated his memory each time they led an action.

Such reflections were all too painful. I had to stop. I got up and started to exercise. It felt good. That day I worked out for an hour and a half.

• **Chapter 30** •

The famous Dr. Julio Cesar Bottari came to talk to me, but he appeared somewhat furtive. "Nidia," he began, "I'm going to write a book based on the life of a young man who comes from a peasant family. He gets help from his uncle in order to study and then becomes a guerrilla fighter. He changes his mind ten years later, after he has been in all the war zones and is a member of the leadership of the FMLN. I need you to help me describe how life is at the front, what you do. Imagine, I don't even know how you build a *tatu* [hut], but I think it would be useful to explain in the book."

"You should consult the files of the intelligence service; that way you can find out everything they have on the subject. I can't help you," was my reply.

"But Nidia, the problem is that I don't have access to those files. My life is simply the medical profession. I've been working here for thirty years. I'm the chief of medical and nursing personnel and I head the infirmary. My job has nothing to do with investigations. That's why I would like someone like you, who has been personally involved in the war, to tell me about it. How do you survive? How do you make things? How do you feel about living that way?"

He kept asking me to provide him with information for the book. I was sure it was a book about Miguel Castellanos. He talked to me as if I didn't know who he was, as if I weren't aware of everything he had said and done.

"Is this your only job?" I asked.

"No, I'm also the chief of neurology at Social Security, at the Psychiatric Hospital and at the Rehabilitation Center. I also have a private practice in the Duke building. I write. I've written several books, *Sexology of the Priesthood* and *A Child's Memoirs*. I'll bring copies for you. Now I want to write about the guerrilla who grows tired of fighting."

I stared straight at him. His attitude was so cynical that he avoided looking me in the eye. He had told me once that he had been politically progressive in the past, and part of the student movement. He said he had known many of the revolutionaries – he had even dared ask me about some of them and their present whereabouts! There were times I wanted to just scream at him, to shout as I had done the first day, that he was an assassin and that I could not stand the sight of him.

I had first met him in 1973, when I was studying psychology. The university had just re-opened after the military occupation by the Molina regime, and the government had placed reactionary elements and informers among the administrative personnel. Bottari was placed in the Department of Neurophysiology. We saw him as a cop, and fought to get rid of him. The entire student body participated in the fight, and we won. I was one the officers of the Association of Psychology Students. Bottari either did not remember me, or was playing dumb. The one he remembered was Miguel Castellanos, and he hated him. He had once said to me, "That Miguel, he can't even be a decent trouble-maker."

I remember the day that he walked into my cell for the first time, so full of confidence. I think it was May 6. He introduced himself as my physician and said that I should always come to him first if I had any problems. He asked me if I felt OK emotionally, adding that I should trust him because he was a psychiatrist and was there to help.

He also told me once that the guerrillas had targeted him because at some point a man found in a sewer after surviving horrendous tortures had denounced him as the torturer. But he insisted this was not the case, that he had never tortured anyone, and that his role was only to take care of those who were ill. The FMLN had accused Bottari of being responsible for brutal tortures, including some carried out using I.V.'s or electrodes. He was responsible for driving dozens of our comrades insane, some now disappeared. He had played a very active role as a torturer in the regime's secret jails and in the political police.

He always tried to appear as Mr. Nice Guy with me, saying he thought very highly of me because he knew we believed in what we were doing. He only wondered, he said, why it was that the FMLN had turned its back on me and had not asked for me in some of their prisoner exchanges. Perhaps they no longer trusted me, he suggested. Sometimes he would tell me that the FMLN was about to carry out an action on my behalf in order to raise my hopes. But usually he argued that the FMLN had abandoned me and that he could not understand it. He suggested that the day I got out of prison I should simply leave immediately for France.

In the beginning he did not want to disclose the fact that he was a colonel in the Armed Forces. I knew his rank from before my capture. One day, however, one of the nurses stood at attention for him. On another occasion he ordered the cop to open my cell and when he did not immediately obey he shouted, "Don't you know I'm a colonel?"

"Look," I said, "I won't help with your book. When I was under interrogation I informed the intelligence people that there were three reasons why I would not talk: first, my principles; second, our work is compartmentalized and one only knows what is necessary; and third, because I know nothing."

Bottari looked at me without speaking. From that moment on he never asked me again to help with his book. Only once he asked me to recommend him to someone at Legal Aid or someone else who would have pictures showing the damage caused by the army to the civilian population, because he said he only had the pictures that appeared in the national press of the FDR-FMLN violating human rights.

He had a psychopathic personality and was apparently undergoing a political crisis. He had always been linked to those in power, beginning with his affiliation to pro-oligarchy political parties. But now the Christian Democrats were in power and in conflict with other powerful sectors. Moreover the oligarchy was now fighting within itself. The Nationalist Republican Alliance (ARENA) had just split. Bottari would tell me that he did not feel comfortable any more within national politics and that he did not feel happy working for someone he did not agree with. He said he did not share Duarte's politics, and that he could not stand North Americans – pointing out that he agreed with me on this one point.

"Let me know when you're not feeling well. Have you been feeling nervous lately?" he would enquire.

"No, everything's fine."

I never got to the point of asking him for a tranquilizer, not even during the most difficult moments when I couldn't sleep. I didn't even ask him during those times in May when I was convinced I would go mad. I never let Bottari see me sad or depressed.

No one had ever hated me so subtly as Bottari. I could see the rage in his pale eyes whenever I caught him looking at me. Once he told me that at a small social gathering some very wealthy folks had asked him about me, about my behavior, and that he had told them I was one of those who would die fighting in the trenches.

Because of the pressure from the Red Cross and Medical Aid for El Salvador, Bottari was forced to process the necessary requirements for my treatment by the Military High Command. He dragged his feet through the procedures for obtaining a cast, the forensic diagnosis, the electromyogram, the facilities for the operations, etc...He pretended to be very concerned and have a real interest in my welfare, whereas it was nothing but an act.

He was repulsive. On May 22, when they first came to negotiate an approval for my operation, he had tried to appear to be most interested in having the operation take place whereas, in fact, he was probably the person most responsible for the delay. Karen Parker and Drs. Lemus and Sánchez left the next day without having performed the operation. International pressure to allow the operation grew to such an extent that when Duarte went to the United States Congress in June 1985, there were members of congress who wanted to know why he would not allow it; and so he was forced to commit himself at the time. True to form, he did not keep his promise. It would take four months of struggle and pressure from the solidarity movement before the microsurgery was allowed.

Since I knew Bottari was a psychiatrist, I reproached him for his lack of interest when I reported to him how at night I could hear the screams of *compañeros* in prison who seemed to be going mad, or maybe already were. They would shake the bars of the gates, sometimes calling for people, sometimes even calling me. I wasn't completely sure whether this was real, or if it was the product of my own anxiety and impotence since I could do nothing to help them.

One night a young man, tall, thin, and good-looking, was taken out of interrogation and put in Cell 17. It hurt so much to see him and then to hear him scream out through the bars, to the wall, "Silvana! Silvana! Don't touch Silvana! Silvana! Silvana! Don't beat her up!" Another time I heard one of those in the cell rattle the gate and shout, "Don't let the baby cry! Don't let him cry!"

After the assassination of Doroteo Gómez Arias in prison the International Red Cross sent a psychiatrist as a delegate to all the jails. He was a specialist in the investigation of psychological and emotional torture. I told him what I had seen and heard. I also mentioned that one of the ways in which they would pressure and harass political prisoners still in interrogation was to send homosexuals to their cells, sometimes dressed as women. One of these instances had occurred in August. He took note and appeared very interested, saying he would bring it before others. Bottari, on the other hand, reacted with indifference. What else could one expect of such an accomplice in this terror?

Part Five

La Palma:
the negotiations
and the
Church

• Chapter 31 •

"The Engineer says that if you want to see him, he will come; you just need to send for him," Dr. Callejas, vice-minister of justice, told me.

What cynicism! I thought. "Tell him that next time I talk to him it will be under different circumstances, not in this prison. There's nothing to talk about right now." Archbishop Rivera had written him a letter which briefly described my circumstances. Under those conditions I was not willing to talk to Duarte, as I outlined in my letter to the archbishop:

National Police Headquarters
June 25, 1985
Monsignor Arturo Rivera y Damas
Archbishop of San Salvador:

I greet you respectfully, hoping that upon the receipt of this letter you find yourself successful in your pastoral work. I hope that you continue to work to overcome the problems that we must confront in this country on a daily basis, and that you find the faith, hope, and energy to do so.

Monsignor, I'm writing to solicit your intervention in favor of my request that I be transferred from the National Police Headquarters to the women's prison at Ilopango. I am requesting this of my own free will for two reasons:

1) I am isolated here at the National Police Headquarters, locked up for twenty-three hours a day, with a permanent guard stationed in front of my cell.

2) Although since my status was changed I am allowed visitors, my relatives and acquaintances are afraid to come here because of the threats and attacks which they, especially my mother, have received. My emotional

support right now depends directly on humanitarian organizations such as the International Red Cross or the Legal Aid Office.

In hope that you will assist me in securing my transfer,

Respectfully yours,

M. Valladares de Lemus

I had been forewarned of the visit of Dr. Callejas through a message from my mother and by Colonel Revelo. I was glad to see her, despite her political affiliation to the Christian Democrats. I was able to deliver another letter to her, also demanding my transfer to Ilopango.

Barracks of the National Police
June 25, 1985
Dr. Dina Castro v. de Callejas
Vice-Minister of Justice of El Salvador:

I greet you respectfully. I'm writing this letter to request your assistance in processing my transfer from the National Police Headquarters to the prison at Ilopango, the women's section. I'm requesting this transfer because that is where political prisoners such as myself should be.

As you know, I have been at the N.P. since May 4, being held over at the request — from that time — of Colonel Melara Vaquero, First Judge of the military system. During my stay here, I have been treated however it has suited the government, both during the interrogation stage, and now as a "hold over"...

Dr. Callejas told me clearly that it would be difficult to obtain the transfer to Ilopango and that, ultimately, the decision would rest with the judge assigned to my case who had not yet been named. She asked me to understand that the government could not send me to Ilopango because they could not guarantee my safety there. Maybe I would be taken to Santa Ana, to the prison of the Second Infantry Brigade, where I would have a larger cell, like an apartment. She told me that before coming she had had to inform "the Engineer" about her visit. She had had to ask Duarte to see the visit as a humanitarian gesture and an act of consideration for my mother, who had been her friend. She mentioned that although she had known me well during the time I had taught her flower arranging, she had not recognized me during the negotiations at La Palma.

She was one of the few friends that my mother had been able to talk to and who at least had been sympathetic. Some of my close relatives, on the other hand, demanded that I give up the struggle before they would consider helping in any way. They told my mother that I was an embarrassment to the family.

Images of Duarte, my mother, friends, and family flashed before me. My head was swimming. I closed my eyes. Relax, I told myself.

My mother had been a political ally of Dr. Callejas. She had even allowed her house to be used for Christian Democrats' meetings, and was a good friend of Doña Melita, Duarte's mother. My little sister had been at school for several years with Duarte's niece, the daughter of his brother, Rolando, and she had spent a lot of time at their house. It was because of this network of relationships that I attended, in May 1983, an intimate dinner for Silvia Duarte, my sister's friend, who was getting married. That was the first time I found myself seated across the table from Duarte.

Maybe he recognized me when we met again at the La Palma negotiations, but he didn't bat an eyelid. Later I learnt that when North American journalists had asked him about the mood at the talks he had said everything had been fine except for the way in which I had stared at him. I think Rey Prendes, a key figure in Duarte's Christian Democratic government, must have felt the same way since my family occasionally socialized with him also.

Perhaps it was these close family relations that had led my mother to write to Duarte to plead my case. My poor mother! At least she tried. Among other things she told him that I was not a terrorist, that I had been moved to fight injustice by my noble feelings. She asked him to allow the medical care offered by various governments. She was shattered by his uncompromising response, in which he repeated the same accusation that I was a terrorist.

San Salvador
June 4, 1985
Doña Mina de Valladares
Hand Delivery

Dear Doña Valladares:

I have received your letter in which you express your feelings as a mother for your daughter, María Marta Valladares, or "Commander Nidia Díaz" as she is known in the organizations of those who have chosen to take up arms.

I have taken into account your concern for your daughter's health, and I have requested the medical records so that I may inform myself of the situation and take appropriate measures.

A few days ago I found out that unprincipled persons have been calling you to threaten you, and that there has even been gunfire aimed at your house. I have asked the National Police to set up guard and to provide you with appropriate protection.

As far as your daughter's case is concerned, you must understand that she was captured in combat and with a weapon in her hand. It becomes impossible to classify her as anything but one of the insurgents, something which she freely acknowledges.

I appreciate all your comments concerning my efforts to bring about a national dialogue and move towards democracy. I hope my efforts will serve to convince people like your daughter, and all those who have taken up arms to subvert the social order because of their ideology, that the road of violence only serves to engender more deaths, hatred, and increased violence, and that the road to democracy can be a genuine vehicle for achieving social peace.

I hope that you will be able to put some love in your

daughter's heart — love, to replace the hatred that has moved her to take such a destructive path.
May God guide you,

José Napoleón Duarte

The ironies of life! Months later, the FMLN captured Inés Duarte, his daughter. In exchange for her freedom, they demanded the release of political prisoners, myself among them. She is older than me by a couple of years. We are both mothers, but in my case no one seemed concerned that I too had a child. In her case, it was one of their strongest arguments. But she was more than an innocent mother and daughter. Inés was a very active member of the Christian Democratic party and worked on their publicity. What's more, she directed their press campaigns during elections and was in charge of a radio station. Nevertheless, they tried to deny all her political activity and dissociated her from any responsibility. I, on the other hand, was accused of every possible crime; I was everything from a delinquent to a terrorist.

It annoyed me each time that Duarte commented on my situation; it bothered me more than what other people said. Maybe it was because of everything I've explained. Or maybe because in 1972, when he was the presidential candidate and Ungo his vice-presidential nominee, I had been a poll worker for the National Opposition Union (UNO). I was already in the guerrilla movement, so I carried out this work as a cover. Or maybe it was because in 1971 I had known people of the Christian Democratic Party, when I worked with a community action group out of the mayor's office.

One morning, some time in 1985 while I was still imprisoned, Duarte gave a breakfast press conference and announced that I was heading the strike at the National Waterworks Administration. People could not figure out why he would link me to that strike. He appeared to be obsessed with my case to the point where he believed that I could lead such a strike even from jail, even if this cast serious doubts about the state's security apparatus.

When the negotiations at La Palma ended, I saw Duarte seated on the stairs inside the church. He was holding his head in his hands. I was talking with Rey Prendes, minister for culture and communication. It was raining, and he had remarked, "I suppose you are used to walking in the rain."

"No, we'll never get used to it," I said. "Rain is simply something we must endure. But whenever we can we carry a tarp or plastic and if it's possible, we find cover. We are human beings too."

We were next to a window with grates; the hands of the people outside were extended through the grates like blooming flowers. They were eager to greet the delegation of the FMLN.

Duarte was watching us, perhaps wondering what Rey Prendes and I were talking about. He had a thoughtful, inquisitive expression. He appeared quite lost.

At the negotiation table Duarte and Rubén Zamora sat face to face for the first time in many years. Zamora had been a leader of the Christian Democrats' youth group, which took a principled stand and broke with the party after it insisted on remaining in power as part of the Christian Democratic junta in 1980. They later founded the Popular Social Christian Movement (MPSC) which, together with the National Revolutionary Movement (MNR) and other sectors formed the Democratic Revolutionary Front (FDR) on April 18, 1980.

I noticed Duarte also watching Ungo from the steps. Maybe he recalled those days in 1971 and 1972, when the Christian Democratic Party and the Nationalist Democratic Union joined together in the National Opposition Union. How far apart they were now! So much had happened in all those years! In those days Duarte stood on a platform for democracy and independence for El Salvador, aiming to alleviate the misery and the condition of backwardness and exploitation of our people.

Various U.S. governments sought to exploit Duarte's political background and his image as an "honest democrat," who had himself been the victim of electoral fraud and repression. He had been exiled from 1972 to 1980, but during those years he underwent a political metamorphosis. By 1980 nothing remained of his progressive politics. He became deaf and blind to the needs of his own people.

In 1980, after a coup by the junta, Duarte returned to the country. Though he was well aware that an alliance between the

Christian Democrats and the Armed Forces would simply provide better cover for the massacres that were taking place, he allied himself to the most reactionary military sectors because he wanted to become part of the junta. Some Christian Democrats realized that the junta was the facade for increasingly brutal repression, and proposed to withdraw from the government. In contrast, Duarte compromised himself even more, resisting all warnings and pleadings. He continued to move his party towards deeper involvement with those who were exploiting his people, thereby becoming complicit in the genocide.

So there he was, still sitting on the steps. Maybe, I thought, he realized that the FMLN would never lay down the arms of the people, that it was foolish of him to have made the proposal for amnesty, and that he was wrong to equate peace with our surrender. Perhaps he recognized how his government had represented a continuing string of failed promises and frustrations. That was why the FDR-FMLN had become the biggest threat to his plans. We were – and still are – the only ones capable of bringing about the necessary reforms. Perhaps he knew that despite its populism his government had solved nothing, but if anything, had exacerbated the situation. His memory of those nine long years since the UNO Alliance must have given him worse nightmares still.

As I watched Duarte on those church steps, I pondered: How much moral fortitude will he need to take the correct courageous, and patriotic reforms which he knows might cost him his life? He would have to disobey Reagan and search for a Salvadoran solution. Crouching there on the steps, it seemed as if the whole situation weighed too heavily on him already.

Then, in an instant, he resumed his role of commander of the Armed Forces, standing next to Vides Casanova, the minister for defense, in the midst of the military butchers, listening to their instructions, making preparations to continue the war.

• Chapter 32 •

When the talks ended in La Palma, Vides Casanova approached us while we were still in the church. "Do you have any children?" he asked.

Didn't he believe we were human beings too? I thought. I wanted to reply and tell him how painful it was to be away from our children. But I only said, "Yes, we all have children."

He said he also had children and began to talk about them. He asked me where I was from. When I told him I was from San Salvador, he seemed surprised.

Here in prison, I learnt to relate more to the soldiers. The situation was very clearly defined: I was their prisoner of war; they were my captors. Two opposing sides. I was confronted with the problem seeing their faces every day. For them, was I simply their trophy, their prisoner, or a nuisance?

Since General Maximiliano Hernández Martínez's rise to power in 1932, the Salvadoran Armed Forces have sustained the country's agribusiness, the power brokers, mainly the oligarchy. Today they are the backbone of the U.S. intervention. Despite this, historically the army has not been a monolithic armed institution. There are different elements within it: a more "pro-oligarchic" sector, another more dependent on the United States, and some constitutionalists who have been very much weakened and isolated. The first two, the large majority, favor U.S. aid. They know that without it, they would perish more quickly. The military caste's well-being and self-improvement is based on corruption and the crumbs from the table of the United States. Some private business sectors have accused them of incompetence in conducting the war since military personnel have shown greater interest in lining their own pockets than winning the war.

During the course of the war, a process of breakdown within the army has taken place, through corruption, vandalism, and desertion. Changes in the command as well as the lower ranks have occurred, among both soldiers and officers. In one instance a pro-oligarchist, Sigifrido Ochoa, commander of Military Detachment No. 2, requested Duarte's resignation. The head of the Air Force, General Bustillo, also joined this call.

The Pentagon has succeeded in running the Salvadoran Armed Forces. Its concept of counter-insurgency has dominated the thinking of the field officers and the reorganization of its structure and training. Colonel García, minister for defense, was removed from office in 1983 as part of this process and replaced by Vides Casanova, who was more servile to the United States.

I used to believe that direct military rule was the most criminal form of dictatorship. Now, after seeing Duarte in power, I have a different perspective. Only the political language and civilian clothes masked the true nature of Duarte's government. The traditional military dictatorships were certainly more cynical, more overt. Duarte and Christian Democracy, as a new type of dictatorship, have demagogy, rhetoric, and deceit as the fulcrum of their policies. But it is no less oppressive or criminal than previous regimes.

My first contact with the military took place in a social context, from which I learnt a lot. My brother-in-law, my older sister's husband, was in the Salvadoran Air Force, which allowed me to visit military installations despite the fact that I was already involved in underground political activity. Two of my mother's house guests were having affairs with soldiers. In addition, my mother's last few jobs had involved dealings with some soldiers. And on top of this, one of my first cousins was studying at the Gerardo Barrios Military School and had joined the operational forces. At times I gave him a ride to the military school in my car, which allowed me to establish different relationships with some of the young soldiers.

They never suspected me, not even during a birthday dinner for my brother-in-law on December 30, 1983. During the dinner, the officers received word of the FMLN attack on the El Paraíso barracks. They left very concerned while I smiled and practically glowed with happiness. Occasionally they talked to me about many aspects of the war, and their views on it. I would only listen, although I desperately wanted to counter their arguments. Sometimes, I limited myself to appearing indifferent or apathetic. Other times, we talked about what the army meant to them and I carefully absorbed what they had to say.

I learnt to despise the brutality of the military as represented by Colonel Mario Velásquez, known as *El diablo* [the Devil]. He was my great-aunt's brother-in-law. He often boasted of the punishments to soldiers he had ordered and atrocities he had committed against the Honduran people during the 1969 war between Honduras and El Salvador. I also heard talk about him and these stories from others.

Obviously there are soldiers who do not want to see the nation sold out to the U.S. – not many, but some. During the 1981 offensive, the barracks in the west rose up and some officers, such as Mena Sandoval, joined the guerrilla ranks. There was also the constitutionalist uprising against the 1972 electoral fraud and the progressive coup d'etat against General Romero in 1979. Thousands of soldiers have been tricked, or drafted into obligatory military service. Monsignor Romero appealed to those young men, when he said "...I beg you, I implore you, I order you, in the name of God, stop the repression!"

In prison, I had no choice but to relate to them. They were there whenever I went out for some sun. Those who couldn't talk directly, would watch me. One day a lieutenant approached and asked me how long I thought I'd be there.

"According to your laws, about thirty years," I told him.

"Oh, it won't be that long," he said.

"Well then, maybe about fifteen."

"Maybe two or five years," he told me. "Do you know that ARENA wants to try you in a military court?"

"They can do that, they can shoot me too."

Lieutenant Serpas arrived, jeering as he asked why I was eating honey and garlic.

"So I'll live longer," I answered.

Others also spoke to me, saying, "Nidia, you must be someone important. You have a radio, and are allowed the newspapers and personal packages; the Red Cross comes to see you, they bring you cigarettes, and your family sends you things." They told me how the officers, especially the commanding officers, joked among themselves, saying "Let's see who gets himself caught by the FMLN so he can be exchanged for Nidia."

Once, during my interrogation, the captain in charge mentioned that he had been shot by the FMLN and didn't want that to happen to him again. Later, in anger, he told me he wished I had been killed.

• **Chapter 33** •

The shadow of the bars was reflected on the wall. In a few minutes, it would be July 28. It surprised me how even here time still passed. I was told that I would be allowed newspapers, but still, none had arrived. This suspension of my right to be informed was most inopportune. I had fought hard for it and was therefore not prepared to give in without a fight.

Despite my weak state, the result of a bad cold, I had fasted the day before in solidarity with Father Miguel D'Escoto, the Nicaraguan foreign minister, who had been on a hunger strike for several days to protest against the contra-war against Nicaragua. In this way I felt part of international solidarity.

I tossed and turned. I couldn't sleep on the narrow mattress. The visit by Monsignor Gregorio Rosa Chávez was a real surprise. I had been expecting a visit from the archbishop's office, but not at night.

I was exercizing when I saw him standing next to my cell. Everyone seemed surprised by his appearance, even Revelo. I had almost no contact with him after we met in 1971; he was the brother of a *compañero* in one of the Christian movements. I probably attended his clerical ordination in San José de la Montaña. I was wary of him because of his political views. However, his visit wasn't entirely unexpected as he had come in response to the letter I had recently written to Monsignor Rivera y Damas. In the letter, I described the unjust, arbitrary, and illegal action of the Military High Command in holding me in police precincts in a cell adjoining the interrogation rooms, and other violations of my rights.

July 9, 1985

Monsignor Arturo Rivera y Damas
Dr. Julio Samayoa (Minister of Justice)
Jorge Serrano (Judge of the Military Court of the First
    Instance)
Colonel Revelo (National Police Chief)

...and to the Human Rights Commission, that the local officials of the Security Corps do not meet conditions by indefinitely holding a political prisoner in prison; there are penal centers with special areas to centralize political prisoners, such as in Ilopango and Mariona.

I am being held at the National Police Headquarters under harsh conditions which is damaging me psychologically and affecting my moral integrity and revolutionary dignity, not only because of what I mentioned previously (isolation and no visitors), but also for the following reasons:

1) My holding cell adjoins the cell where interrogations take place.

2) For me, irregardless of my will, it is psychological torture to see blindfolded prisoners constantly go by (in the hall in front of my cell), coming and going to interrogations, as well as to hear the interrogations when every psychological mechanism is used, such as arrogant, shouting voices, sudden pounding on the table, placing and dragging chairs (all of which I experienced during my interrogation). The prisoners are my people and it is painful to witness their suffering.

3) I have been informed that when the prisoners are interrogated, the security men tell them that I say I know them or that the documents which were found on me contain information that connects them with the FMLN. As I am in a security institution unable to speak for myself some people may believe such slander.

4) Being in National Police Headquarters has given rise to abuses, such as deceitful interrogations, including when a detective came to show me four photographs of a

woman and asked me several times if I knew her.

5) Because I have certain privileges not permitted the temporary prisoners I do not have the opportunity to explain my situation and conditions to them.

6) When I go out for some sun and fresh air, I am a "spectacle," and attract the attention of people, who end up seeing me as being privileged. That is understandable considering my condition and situation.

7) Because my right to purchase and read newspapers has been taken away.

For all those above-mentioned reasons, and as a show of repudiation of this disrespect and arbitrariness, as of today I will reject all special food I am given here and will only accept the regular food that is eaten by all prisoners.

After eighty-three days in prison, my only recourse is once again to request that steps are taken to transfer me to the Ilopango Penal Center.

M. Valladares M. de Lemus

After further outlining my demands and responding to the monsignor's questions on my conditions, the conversation came to an end. Rosa Chávez said goodbye with his characteristic coldness. When he left, Revelo, Serpas, López Dávila and other officers were waiting for him. I managed to hear him telling them that I should be removed to another cell or otherwise they should suspend the interrogations next door.

"We'll see what we can do. We'll switch her cell. The situation with her is really delicate," the officers replied.

The tall, thin silhouette of Rosa Chávez disappeared in the hallway, one more shadow in the darkness. The other prisoners' faces peered out from behind the bars, reflecting their apprehension, their hands signaling, asking what was happening and why the monsignor had come. I signaled to them that the visit was unimportant, that nothing would change. One learns to figure these things out. I knew they would not move me, and although there were fewer interrogations next door, they did not stop altogether.

While falling asleep during one of those supposedly nonexistent questionings, I thought of Rosa Chávez. The last time I had seen him had been October 15, 1984, at La Palma, when we held the first negotiations with the government. I recalled that when we entered we saw the government's representatives with their backs to the people, seated around the meeting table in the center of the church. They all stood and greeted Monsignor Rivera y Damas and then our delegation, which was headed by Dr. Ungo and Commander Fermán Cienfuegos.

We sat facing their delegation, looking out at the people. Then the door was closed. Even though they could no longer see us our people knew that all the power that exists in El Salvador was represented there, and that our delegation was there as the true representative of their interests.

To begin, Rivera y Damas said a prayer and then crossed himself, as we all did. The presence of the archbishop as an intermediary in this dialogue gave the Church a new legitimacy. It had responded to the demands of the time: through the dialogue, it had taken on the political commitment to help resolve the conflict.

When Rosa Chávez saw that no one was taking the bread and coffee which had been served, he approached each one of us quietly and whispered in our ear, "Eat, don't be afraid; we prepared this food in the archbishop's house."

I also remember that the government delegation was drinking cold tomato juice. In keeping with their lifestyle, they were recovering from hangovers from the night before. They were nervous, their faces were inexpressive. Apparently they were not listening to us. We had forced them to sit down to negotiate independent of their own political maneuvering. It was to be a long, difficult, and complex process.

At one end of the table, facing Rivera y Damas, sat Rosa Chávez in front of a typewriter; he was the recording secretary. Next to him sat Monsignor Cabrera, bishop of the Diocese of Santiago de María, who was there representing the Vatican Nuncio. The joy, the songs, and the slogans from outside the church filled the air. We could feel the anxiety of the crowd, around 50,000 people, who wanted to come into the church where the dialogue was taking place; they wanted to know what was going on.

In spite of the repression, the people had come to La Palma. They had to pass through many checkpoints, but they still came to stand beside us and cheer the FDR-FMLN. For us it was eloquent proof of their support. The meeting had barely been announced when people began to organize and to flood the media of the country with their pronouncements in favor of the dialogue. They wanted a permanent and stable peace, and expressed their desire for an end to U.S. intervention.

Adolfo Rey Prendes, minister of culture, was obviously nervous and spilled a glass of water over my papers. So was Duarte, who kept reaching in and out of his briefcase unable to locate the documents he was looking for. He presented his peace proposal: simply, that we surrender. He had already copied and distributed the document. In violation of the ground rules established for the meeting, it was already being read over the air on Radio National.

Abraham Rodríguez, first in line to succeed the president, was also part of the government delegation, together with Vides Casanova and Fortín Magaña. Duarte called them "the president's team." Rodríguez kept looking at us mockingly from behind his glasses, and insisted that he would much rather listen to the "commanders from the mountains" than to the civilians who were there.

During the preceding nights and days, as we crossed the mountains, fields, and rivers, we had marched so confidently towards this meeting, full of certainty that this mission would be a success for us and for our people.

A scramble of echoes and shadows reached my cell with the damp cold of dawn. Screams broke the silence. My muscles tightened and I felt my blood rise. I shut my eyes, squeezing hard to blot out the images. There was an interrogation starting in the next cell.

> I've had enough
> I can feel their pain
> it's my pain
> I see their sad eyes
> behind the blindfolds

eyes filled with tears
and dignity.
One by one
they come
in columns
I can feel their anger and hate
in the beating of my heart.
I feel their suffering,
their exhaustion,
their hope.

Are they courageous or cowardly?
Are they masters or slaves?
Do they feel cornered?
Oh, this interminable time,
endless interrogations!
Oh, sleepless weeks
and months!
The comings and goings,
playing blind man's bluff.
I played,
I'm still playing...

I asked myself many times why it was so important for the FMLN to establish a dialogue with the government. Why on earth did we insist on dialogue with such an enemy.

• Chapter 34 •

How can we make peace with these torturers and assassins? Could I really question this? We seek a dialogue because we seek peace, because we believe in the possibility of a political solution for the conflict in El Salvador. That's why the FDR-FMLN has proposed, time after time, numerous options for negotiation.

In November 1984 the FMLN presented a proposal for a political solution to be implemented in three stages. But all our initiatives were systematically blocked or obstructed in some way. The regime was not willing to give up anything and set their sights solely on our military defeat. Over the years, the FMLN has defeated one by one the various stages of the counter-insurgency plan. At different times, government spokespeople have had to recognize that without U.S. military aid they would have been defeated long ago. We outlined this in the negotiations at La Palma, when we explained how the army has been progressively losing its national identity and becoming an instrument of the United States. I remember the expressions on the faces of Vides Casanova, Duarte, and Monsignor Rivera y Damas when we were able to get our point across. Abraham Rodríguez went so far as to acknowledge that the United States was paying them one and a half million dollars a day to wage war on their behalf.

Using different tactics, the Duarte government tried to confuse national and international public opinion, creating the impression that the FMLN didn't want to continue the dialogue. But we continued pressing to have a third meeting, one with no preconditions. We had proposed it for April 1985, but it was a long time before the government responded.

Once during the La Palma negotiations Duarte became very nervous and rose from the table to consult with Abraham Rodríguez. We were proposing that a forum be held so that all democratic sectors could have the opportunity to participate in the dialogue. The same thing happened when we proposed a truce; he became restless, as did Vides Casanova. They told us to forget any ideas of forums or truces, because they would have serious problems as a result. It was clear they had not come with the intention of seriously discussing any specific proposals. We agreed to set up a joint commission to continue working on the issue and prepare proposals for mechanisms to achieve peace and to humanize the conflict. Later, in Ayagualo, the procedural norms for the functioning of this special commission were established. This commission, however, never met.

When we parted at La Palma they went so far as to say, "Good-bye, Commanders. We wish you well."

Monsignor Rosa Chávez had told us we would have a press conference at the conclusion of the talks. We thought it would be private, and were totally surprised when they simply opened the large doors of the church and we found ourselves facing the multitudes. Ungo and Fermán said a few emotional words. Perhaps under different circumstances we might have taken greater advantage of the opportunity, but we were all overcome by emotion. To make things worse, the international organizations who had been present were pressuring us to leave as soon as possible. One had to have lived through that moment to fully understand its significance. The crowd was chanting and cheering for our delegation. We felt even more certain that the will for peace was theirs, that it came from them. We were simply representing that will.

As for me, I had never been on a platform facing so many people. The kind of activity I had usually carried out had not permitted it. At that moment I was face to face with my people, *as myself!* It was a coming together for them and for us. I left feeling even more certain that all the democratic forces were heading down the same path towards constructing a different kind of government, a truly democratic, representative government. This was the future, whether or not Duarte agreed to continue the negotiations.

I was startled from sleep by the interrogator's shouting. I was overcome with sadness to wake once again to the sounds of that horror. I thought the knot in my throat would explode.

> I feel hatred, disdain,
> for you arrogant enemy.
> Your demanding voices,
> your mockery, your emotional pressures
> your noises, your sudden blows
> your hoods, your electric shocks.
>
> The more humble your victims,
> the more you trample upon them
> their hand shakes as they sign
> the confession you prepared for them.
>
> For two nights and more
> screams echo in the narrow, darkened cells.

Some even lose their minds –
all balance broken
and all human promise and dignity
destroyed
gone forever.

I guessed it was about four in the morning. Rays of light from the hall lamp shone into my cell. I stared at the woman on horseback. I longed to return to the mountains, to shift the battlefield away from that place, to breathe fresh air through every pore. To live again.

And the dialogue? Duarte had broken it indefinitely, continuing to make concessions to those with money and power, promising them he would not negotiate with us. His real character, that of a demagogue, had come to the fore. There was nothing left of that "great statesman" who had addressed the United Nations in 1984.

• Chapter 35 •

The pressure of the silence weighed heavily upon me, inspite of the noises from the construction machinery and the air hammers outside. They had isolated me further in those last few days. No one was brought to the adjoining cells any more. They used to bring the women prisoners to Cell 19. However, when they discovered I was giving them food and communicating with them, they took the women to the smaller cells on the floor below. The only time they opened the cell next to mine now was when the delegates from the Red Cross came to talk to the prisoners.

I was outside getting some sun when Serpas arrived. He always provoked me into a discussion. Very subtly he would try to lower my morale. This time, he told me that the decision to take me to the National Police Headquarters had been a political decision. He told me that many of the officers were angry that I had not been killed. I was surprised at his candor when one day he said bluntly he thought I should have been shot.

Yet, the next time I saw him, he would be so affable! The man was insufferable! "Look, kid, from now on you won't see anyone blindfolded in front of your cell, nor will you hear any more interrogations in the cell next to yours," he said, awaiting my reaction.

"You're doing that because Monsignor Gregorio Rosa Chávez came."

"By the way, why did he come?" he asked, trying not to appear too interested.

"To hear my confession."

"To hear your confession?"

"Yes," I said curtly.

"So you still have faith in the Church?"

"Well, it's a neutral institution. They work from a humanitarian perspective. We respect the Church and we think you should respect it, too."

"The Church is neutral?" he asked, as if in doubt.

"Yes, of course."

"Look," he said, changing the subject, "I think if you ever get out of here, you shouldn't come back to the city. You're too well-known and too easily identified."

"Don't worry," I said. "The FMLN leadership will know where to put me, and if they decide that I should be in the city, well, the city it is."

"I would recommend that you go abroad."

Serpas continued to chat. He told me that I could watch television whenever I wanted and that they had very good videos. He recommended "Kathy, the cocoon," which showed people having sex. He kept on talking. I looked at him in disgust and walked away. I returned to my cell.

As I passed in front of the other prisoners' cells I made myself smile as I did not want to let my anger show in front of them. I always felt I should try to lift their spirits. There were times when I could not stand to be near anyone except them. The guard who was walking alongside me noticed the change in my expression. I was upset that the other prisoners weren't allowed to go out in the sun, though after they were transferred to Mariona or Ilopango they would be able to go outside every day, for a long time. I smiled because I had been able to see them, because they said hello to me, because they would all soon be out of this place.

"Hi, how are you getting on?" they asked.

"I'm fine. In Mariona you'll be able to catch some sun. The political prisoners' organization won that right for you," I reassured them. Back in my cell again, I started to hum "Guantanamera" and the song began to rise in me...

Guantanamera,
guajira guantanamera,
guantanamera,
guajira guantanamera.

la la larala larala
la la lala larala...

I changed the lyrics around a little. I just felt like singing.

I listened to the news again: the contra mercenaries in Nicaragua had wounded eighteen mothers, eight of whom had died, and one soldier in Matagalpa, and had begun to attack Estelí. The contra were operating from Honduras, trained and armed by the United States. They had already been strategically defeated. The Sandinista People's Army had been able to contain them more and more. The Contadora nations were meeting in Panama. The presidents of Uruguay and Colombia were looking to create a support group for Contadora. They all supported a negotiated solution for Central America that would be an obstacle for U.S. aggression. Events were moving so fast! Keeping mental lists of all this helped me break down my isolation. So much to think about and discuss, even if only with myself.

That night I re-read what I had written about Janeth Samour. I thought about her so often during my interrogation, while I was carried about on the stretcher, and later back in my cell. I had never realized how much I cared about her. There were so many *compas* in the FMLN, but often I did not realize the extent of my attachment to them.

There, in jail, I realized that Janeth symbolized for me all the disappeared, all those who did not have the chance I did to survive. While I was on the stretcher in the helicopter, I was convinced I would end up as one of the disappeared. Such is life! So many things in prison brought forth painful memories of

Janeth: when I ate, I wondered if she had gone hungry; when I lay under the blankets on cold nights, I imagined her suffering in the cold without even a sheet to cover her. When I moved and my wounds hurt, I thought of how they might have tortured her, perhaps breaking some of her bones. I usually laugh a lot; but when I laughed during that time, either with other prisoners or when I received visits from international organizations, I remembered that she must have cried a lot, as I did – quietly, to herself. My capture had been acknowledged; she simply vanished, all alone, never to enjoy the sunshine as I did now. It was odd, I always felt her close. I sensed she would have kept her spirits high to the end.

When I first met her she wore her blond hair long and loose. I remembered her during the period of mass mobilizations and peasant organizing in 1974. We met again during the restructuring of the underground networks. There had been so many times when we had gone out to talk, to share and celebrate some success in our military operations! And many other times when we had discussed politics and our plans for the urban work. I recalled one meeting with her. I was told to meet someone at a cafeteria where I would be introduced to my contact. When I entered a very refined woman got up from a table, hugged me and said, "Darling! I'm so glad to see you!" I didn't recognize her, she had changed so much.

There in jail, I always felt her presence. By chance alone we had not met the same fate. The fact that I was not disappeared was an exception to the rule. They didn't have to put me in a secret jail, I was the victim of legalized terror. How dare they try to terrorize us! I thought. I was burning with anger. How dare they try to terrorize the workers! Janeth's disappearance enraged me. Her rights were not respected. I would have given part of myself to save her, for her freedom. I calmed myself by remembering that she was not alone. The people, and our vanguard, were with her then and with me now. Maybe, I thought, I will never get out of this place, but then again, maybe I will. Janeth never had that hope. Nevertheless, I felt her there beside me.

I sketched while I thought about her: slender, golden, with handcuffs around her wrists and ankles, blindfolded. I pictured her hands outstretched through the bars, and beyond the bars there was a sun. I had never been in one of the military's secret jails, but I imagined it.

I tortured myself thinking about her. Maybe they kept her naked, or worse...I drifted towards sleep in the midst of the pain. "Good night, Janeth! Good night, Luis."

• **Chapter 36** •

Ten years before, on July 30, 1975, 50,000 of us had filled the streets, workers and students protesting against the repressive measures of the government. On that occasion we were opposing the violation of the Western Student Campus, which the army had raided on the eve of a satirical[1] student parade to commemorate Saint Anne.

The youth were filled with enthusiasm. Colonel Molina was in power and we seized every opportunity to denounce his regime. The regime had warned we would suffer the consequences if we marched out into the streets. But everyone was so enraged that in spite of all the threats, we took to the streets in open defiance. We were organized into three contingents.

The First Infantry Brigade of the National Guard had planned its operations well. When the students advanced, the armored cars confronted them. The first contingent was composed of high school students and many of them were crushed to death. There was generalized panic. It was a confrontation between defenseless people and large sophisticated vehicles.

So many massacres occurred after that. How many more would there be? In 1974, the peasant uprisings in La Cayetana, San Francisco, Tres Calles and Chinamequita were brutally repressed. The system had begun to slide towards fascism. On February 28, 1977, the people took Plaza Libertad. Large sectors of the population had gone out on strike and a general strike was called. People were fighting for their rights. They had voted at the

---

1. In colloquial Spanish: *bufo*. A *bufo* parade was one more form used for the expression of criticisms against the government, their abuse of power and corruption.

polls for the candidates of the National Opposition Union, but the regime had ignored them, using the most blatant fraud in history to impose a military man, Humberto Romero, as the head of the government. He came to power by blood and bayonets, under a state of emergency decree that would last until 1979. They paid a heavy price for that massacre in Plaza Libertad. The more organized sectors fought back and made their presence felt. Even though they had little training and no time to prepare, the popular forces battled all day in San Salvador.

These repressive actions were followed by others in 1979 and 1980, by which time the government's actions constituted open genocide. There was a massacre of protestors on January 22, 1980, and then again during the funeral of Archbishop Romero who had been assassinated on the steps of the cathedral in March of the same year. Then came the butchering at El Mozote in December of 1981, which left 1,000 dead. By then, the war had become widespread and genocide was the central tool of the regime.

Beginning in 1980, the Christian Democrats – the party with which democratic and progressive forces had formed the UNO alliance, one which people had been ready to defend with their lives – had now become the repressive force with Duarte at its head. The massacres continued: Sumpul, Calabozo, Copapayo, and so many others. There will probably be many more before El Salvador is free.

I have seen so much blood flow, and sometimes even been splattered by the blood of those I loved who fell beside me. It is with them, and for them, that we remain determined that our country will decide its own destiny.

On that July day I was in the contingent of marchers that got trapped on the bridge by the Social Security building. The army began to throw tear gas and to spray us with machine-gun fire. It was like my experience in the teachers' union protests some years earlier in 1971. Bullets were flying everywhere. A student leader fell at my side. His name was Carlos Fonseca, a sociology student. The Sociology Students Association was later named after him. There was mass confusion. Many were dying. Many more were wounded, either by the bullets or by the slashes from the knives of the death squad members who had infiltrated among us. Some of us were able to break through the military encirclement and found cover in a parking lot. Salvador Guerra, who is now a commander in the FMLN, was there.

Those of us who survived would never forget this experience which became a turning point in the struggle. On August 1, as we left a memorial mass for sixteen dead and twenty-four disappeared *compañeros*, we took over the cathedral as a coordinating group representing all popular sectors. It was the first time we had done this. We demanded justice be carried out in finding and punishing those responsible for the massacre, the cathedral being a safe platform from which our voices could be heard.

There were about sixty of us: priests, teachers, peasants, students, and workers. I was on the coordinating committee. Many of us would later join the FMLN.

In the midst of this movement, I met Ruth. We did not become fast friends at the time. It was a period of turmoil, characterized by various political differences and organizational disarray. The consolidation of grassroots revolutionary organizations was just beginning, though the five main currents which would later form the FMLN already existed. We spent five years fighting to gain control, to see which among us would win the leadership of the mass movement.

The split between the Revolutionary People's Army (ERP) and the National Resistance (RN) had already taken place. RN was taking on a character of its own. The Revolutionary Worker's Party (PRTC) of El Salvador was coming into its own, evolving out of a nucleus of people who had initially helped found the ERP in 1970-71.

I saw Ruth again in 1984 in Chalatenango. We were both much more mature, and we were living through a period of more encouraging developments than the years 1975-80. I saw her again in 1985 when she spent three days at my camp. Ruth was a member of the central leadership of the Popular Liberation Forces (FPL). We conducted a series of bilateral exchanges which strengthened our strategic perspective and lent some uniformity to the methodology that both organizations were using in our political-military training schools.

She was a very unassuming woman. Far from allowing herself to be demoralized by the death in combat of her sister, Eugenia, she had become even more committed as a result. I admired her as a revolutionary, as a friend, and as a woman. Like everyone else, she had had to leave her three small children behind. It had been months since she'd last seen them, yet she had managed to maintain her family as a strong unit. She was very articulate and sure of herself. Her cheerful manner was contagious. I remember after my return from the negotiations in La Palma I went to give a talk to one of the political training schools. She approached me saying very softly, "Congratulations for having been to the dialogue; you were representing the women. Not only were you there in the name of our vanguard, but you were there to demonstrate the level of participation of all of us as women. You were there for us. Thank you."

And she gave me a kiss. I was very moved by her words. There are times when we ourselves are not aware of the significance of our actions. She was two years younger than I, about my height, slender, pale, with almond colored eyes which stood out in contrast to her flushed cheeks. I always thought her very pretty. Her abilities and qualities made her even more beautiful.

Those days we had spent in the cathedral had been tension filled, but they had fostered qualitative progress in the struggle of our people. There were thousands and thousands of people permanently congregated outside the church. We were kept informed by the *compas*. On the inside, we denounced the repression and reported any new developments in the situation.

The army surrounded the area, but they did not dare attack as they threatened. It was the first time the statue of the World's Saviour, enshrined in the cathedral, was not used in the traditional procession. They had to use an imitation. All regular worship and traditional celebrations at the cathedral were suspended, even though it was the holy period to celebrate the patron saint. Normally, it would have been a time of holidays and carnivals, of games, parades, and floats. That year it was a period of mourning and struggle.

Thousands of women dressed in black marched through the streets of San Salvador, demanding the resignation of the officers responsible in the massacre. Colonel Arturo Armando Molina was again denounced by the people.

The demands of that struggle made possible the coordination

of all the organizations in the movement through the July 30 Committee of Popular Organizations. I remember a meeting we held one night in the basement of the cathedral with Mélida Anaya Montes, the secretary general of the teachers' union. She had come to brief us on developments. The place was tiny and we had to sit on the floor. We formed a circle around a candle so that we could see each other. I had met her earlier, in 1971 during the massive teachers' demonstration.

On the night of August 6, after we had reached an agreement with the Molina government through the mediation of the Church, we left the cathedral. The archbishop at the time was Monsignor Chávez y Gonzalez. The internal coordinating committee met afterwards, at another place, to evaluate what had happened and to plan our next actions.

The July 30 Committee died a slow death. The conditions of disarray that characterized the revolutionary organizations affected it as well. Nevertheless it had been a very important juncture; agendas were drafted for the work of each national sector and each of the organizations, laying out each one's goals and objectives.

It was in this context that the Popular Revolutionary Block was founded, and the divisions inside the United Popular Action Front were exacerbated.

• Chapter 37 •

This July 30, 1985, the situation was different: there was unity in the vanguard and the power and strength of the FDR-FMLN were irrefutable. The war had spread throughout the country.

Student demonstrations continued. A demonstration and meetings were called to commemorate the tenth anniversary of July 30, 1975. The mothers of political prisoners and the disappeared marched together with the students this time, continuing the tradition of laying wreaths at the commemorative plaque on the wall of the Social Security building. The students were also marching to protest the cuts made by the government in the

National University's budget, amid allegations that it was linked to the FMLN and that it was a "terrorist breeding ground." The students marched to the Legislative Assembly to present their demands but they were not granted a meeting.

The government had only recently returned control of the university to the proper authorities. The military troops which had raided and occupied it had ransacked and stolen much of the university's property. But the university had not ceased functioning during that period. It had simply gone into exile, and had survived under very difficult conditions. The campus had been militarized and the university was forced to function outside of its own grounds. Many private universities sprang up to take its place, commercializing education and lowering its technical and scientific standards. Their objective was not the quality but the quantity of graduating technicians so as to magnify their profits. Many students were thus denied their right to an education.

You could feel the upsurge in the struggle everywhere. I knew, even from inside my prison cell, that history was burning outside. A national teachers' strike was taking place, demanding a salary increase. The Workers' Solidarity Committee had presented demands to the Ministry of Labor to resolve the conflict of the water workers.

The struggle had not just flared in my country alone. In Havana, the International Conference on the Third World Debt had been convened. Latin America was looking for a new economic order and more equal standards for commercial exchange. Dr. Ungo and Commander Fermán Cienfuegos were to speak at this conference.

With all this going on outside, I had not been able to sleep for a few nights. The last month had been very important in the political life of the country. Would I spend another July still in prison? I wondered. Where will I be for the seventh anniversary of the Sandinista Revolution on July 19 next year? Where will I commemorate the death of Manuel Federico Castillo, a compatriot who died fighting with the Sandinista Front? Farabundo Martí and Augusto César Sandino, two men of the same blood, with the same destiny. Manuel Federico was there also, united in the one thought, the one will of Central America: to fight until victory.

The last time I had seen Manuel was during the second congress of the PRTC in Honduras, in 1979. He had been very influential in my political development, especially during the popular struggles of 1975 and 1976. He said the influence was mutual. We had many things in common and a real political affinity.

I counted the bars once more. If it depends on the judicial process, I will never get out of here, I thought to myself. Judge Serrano was a member of the judicial establishment and he would never make the decision to transfer me to Ilopango, as it would mean a confrontation with the High Command of the Armed Forces. When he came to see me, he always said he was going to send me to Ilopango and that there was no reason for me to have to undergo a military trial. But the attorney from the Legal Aid office had told me that day that now the judge was not so sure he would transfer me. There was a lot of opposition to my transfer, and he was being criticized for not having issued a quick decision in my case. I became convinced that the only way I would get out would be through my own struggle, through the struggle of the FMLN.

I had turned so many things over in my mind during the day. It was now midnight. It was cold and rainy; the dampness in my cell made it even colder. The last day of July was beginning, and as I did every day, I tried to recall events that had occurred on that same date. Four years before on July 31, the CIA had assassinated the Panamanian nationalist, Omar Torrijos. I thought about how much he had meant to his own people, and to all the progressive anti-interventionist forces in the world. For our movement it meant the loss of a friend, a co-thinker, who had always supported our anti-imperialist struggle. He had been a leader who always defended the interests of his nation against the United States. He represented a stumbling block for the CIA and for the newly-installed Reagan administration. That's why they killed him. That's why they will continue to assassinate people like him.

I thought of the monthly evaluation of our work in the FMLN; the military report said that we had caused 425 casualties in the government's army.

• Chapter 38 •

I was lying back on the floor, exhausted from dancing. After I got the radio, I would tune in Radio Mundo's jazz and rock program at 2 p.m. every Sunday. I danced with bare feet so that the guard would not hear me. I had been able to dance since the cast on my leg had been removed at the end of June. My body would move to the beat of the rhythm; it didn't matter if it was jazz, a waltz, or folk music. I couldn't help but dance.

I still had to be careful, though. I had just had an operation on my right arm and had a cast extending from above my elbow down to my fingers.

I used to dance in the mountains, too. I loved to dance "El Torito Pinto" and the "Guayabo Revolucionario" played by the "Tepeuani" or "Torogoces de Morazán" bands. Sometimes people would improvise, making drums out of tins and percussion instruments out of lamps, combs, and coins.

Going though my daily mental exercise, I asked myself: Who are the people who have helped make history on this day? Ten years ago it was Felipe Peña and Gloria Palacios. Five years ago it was Luis Díaz. I wonder who it will be today, and in the future...Who knows who they will be. Other *compas* will leave their imprint through their example.

Felipe and Gloria had both been personal friends of mine. He was one of the founders of the FPL. Gloria and I had studied psychology together at the university. They were killed while working in the urban underground. The safe house they lived in together in Santa Anita was surrounded by the military. Even though there were hundreds of troops, they never succeeded in taking the house. Gloria and Felipe fought heroically for hours. When he was shot, she escaped by scaling the back wall carrying him on her back, even though she had been wounded as well. We used to call her "Little Chinese Ursula." They captured her behind the wall; they raped her and mutilated her breasts.

I could not go to the funeral because I was working outside of the city, but my mother went to the wake because she had known

159

their parents. In 1972 Felipe used to come over to my house, and, working through "Ursula," reinforced my links with the FPL. By the time he approached me formally about joining the FPL, however, I found myself in a difficult position because I had already begun working with another organization.

The economics students at the university named their association after Felipe. Our military forces, too, named a group of battalions "Commander Felipe Peña Mendoza."

The music kept playing and I felt like dancing again, but the guard had begun to pace the hallway. Once he had stood watching while I danced in the middle of the room with my back to him. He clapped when the music stopped. I was so furious! That time was mine, to enjoy myself. I did not want to share it with my captors. Those moments were a pleasure I was only prepared to share with other prisoners.

I remember Luis, with his characteristic air of serenity, his wide forehead, and his easily wrinkled brow. He reminded me of Lenin. I met him on a December afternoon, when we became part of the same party cell. Together we would carry out many missions, and even though I was older, we got along very well. We became part of the leadership of our organization. Politically, he stood out because of his clear strategic vision and his organizing and propaganda skills; he was very creative. He became secretary general of the Popular Liberation Movement in 1979, and was a member of the leadership of the Revolutionary Coordinating Body for Mass Organizations until the time of his disappearance on August 15, 1980.

After his death, Humberto Mendoza, a member of the Democratic Revolutionary Front (FDR), took his place in the leadership. He, too, was assassinated that same year on November 27. I had known Humberto since 1970 and later we worked together in a coordinating body. I remembered both Luis and Humberto that day. We had all participated in some of the first military actions. As a security measure, we were not allowed to talk; we would simply look at one another. As time passed, we would run into each other occasionally.

Now there is a battalion of FMLN forces that bears Luis's name, and one of our military schools is named after Humberto Mendoza.

We all came to care a great deal for Luis's mother. Three out of her four children had given their lives for the freedom of our people: Adán was killed in combat in 1971; Mauricio disappeared in 1980. She had been driven to the brink of madness, but she always regained her balance. She is still committed to the work, and encourages us with her words and her actions. I thought of so many mothers like her!

The music distracted me and I didn't want to have to think any more. I wanted to relax, to sleep on the cold, barren floor.

• Chapter 39 •

I had a paper butterfly in my cell. I love the natural ones and this one could have almost been real. In the mountains, the *compas* would help me catch them. I would put them in a book after they died. Now I understand them: they must have felt imprisoned, the way I felt at that moment. I guess what I really enjoyed was watching them fly free, like queens of the garden. They're such ugly caterpillars at first, but then, after metamorphosis, they turn into majestic creatures, so beautiful! I particularly like the little ones. In San Miguel, in the month of August, they come together in flower formations. When you go by, they open up and envelop you. It's like being in another dimension.

When I was free in the mountains I would go down to the rivers to bathe. My country has so many rivers of incomparable beauty, large and small. The butterflies would hover over the water, keeping me company. I remember specifically one I saw in Chalatenango: its wings were lilac blue within a black border, and each wing had two red dots. When it flew away, weaving through the air, I could see the black underside of its wings. The dots were white on that side and seemed to have been capriciously sketched with a white pencil; they could have been maps of roads or rivers.

There were also monarch butterflies, dressed in their tiger stripes. One *compa*, who had heard me admiring them, sprained his foot trying to catch one for me. On another occasion I almost fell down the side of a mountain as I was chasing butterflies. Someone caught four for me after that.

There's an insect we call "esperanza," which means hope. People believe it represents good news. One started to fly into my cell with regularity; it would come for a few days, then stay away a few days. I couldn't figure out where it came from; it seemed rather incongruous in that place.

I had put on the white dress the women prisoners had sent me. They frequently sent me their greetings. I would write to them. They had been the first people with whom I had some communication. They were carrying out a campaign for my transfer to Ilopango. Graciela Menjívar, or Rosa Elena Romero, was one of the main leaders. She always sent her regards and good wishes, urging me on. She would share with me the bread her mother sent. How like a sister she was to me! The men had made me a belt, but they were never permitted to send it.

Graciela stood out in the university struggles in 1975. She was a medical student, and elected to the executive committee of the student association, which was called the League for Liberation at the time. I did not see her again for many years, until 1981 to 1983 when we worked together. When the Duarte regime captured her in March 1985, she had become a movement leader. I found her to be a woman of great humanity and dignity. You could sense her revolutionary pride behind that gypsy look. Some interpreted it as haughtiness. Her capacity for organizing work was extraordinary; she was like an ant with a very systematic approach.

I realized it was now September 13, my nephew Germán Armando's birthday. I had lavished a lot of love and attention on him during his first two years of life. Now he was already a young man, studying at the Central American University. He and my sister were forced to leave the country when the regime began to threaten and persecute them.

The guard opened the door. "You have company. Go down."

"Me? Company?" I asked. Who could it be?

"I don't know. I just have orders to take you down."

I entered Serpas's office. A man and a woman were there. He introduced himself as Pastor Ridruejo, human rights reporter at the United Nations. I was surprised. I really was not expecting someone of his stature, and I had only fifteen minutes in which to present my case. I didn't know where to begin.

"Well, you know that I was captured by a U.S. adviser," I started to explain. "From the beginning I claimed my status as a prisoner of war, and even Duarte had to recognize that I had been 'captured' in combat, that I held the rank of commander, and that I had participated in the fighting. I was wounded and spent sixteen days under interrogation, during which I was not given the medical attention I required. During that time, I was forced to go without sleep; the pain killers and first aid I received were not adequate. After four months, because the Red Cross, the Church, and several other governments intervened, I was finally allowed the operation on my arm.

"In addition, my detention here is arbitrary, illegal, and unjust. At this time I am the only prisoner still in isolation, since they will not transfer me to Ilopango. It is my right to go there – even within their judicial framework. Emotional pressures and psychological torture continue. I am kept in the cell next to where they conduct their interrogations, which I can hear at all times of day and night. I have to watch the prisoners as they are taken in and out of violent interrogations. My family has been persecuted, and, like thousands of other people in this country, has been forced to leave.

"I also want it known that Doroteo Gómez Arias was detained here and that he was assassinated by the regime," I concluded.

"Nidia, we can only allow personal testimonies," he remarked, "by the person who has suffered the violations. Besides we already have information about the case you mentioned from other humanitarian sources."

"Commander Hugo was also here," I remembered to add. "I was with him today at Mariona. He recounted his experience for me."

"Look," I continued, "the Duarte regime chose to make an exception in my case. They respected my life and acknowledged my capture only because they could not get away with just disappearing me after the outcry from national and international organizations when they disappeared Janeth Samour and *compañera* Maximina. We're all supposed to be protected under the Geneva Accords, but they never even recognized their detention and refuse to say what happened to those two."

Serpas returned and with great impatience announced our time was up.

• Chapter 40 •

I turned around and left, thinking of what else I could have said, or should have said. Whenever I had such an opportunity I felt desperate to denounce the plight of all the political prisoners. The same thing had happened in August, when Jemera Rone, of Americas Watch, and Maggy Popking, of the Institute of Human Rights of the University of Central America, had come to see me. I realized that I needed to prepare something in writing for these occasions, so that my ideas would be coherent and I could deliver a more complete statement.

I was better organized at the meeting with Legal Aid and when I went before the judge. The fact that there were more than 500 political prisoners under the Duarte dictatorship was sufficient evidence to demonstrate that it was a government which systematically violated political freedoms. Even the Church addressed itself to the issue admitting there were "many people in prison who should not be there, who have been put there primarily for political reasons."

Not only were prisoners being physically and psychologically tortured from the time they were captured, but the abuse continued during the entire period of their detention. Violence against prisoners had increased over the last year. One of these instances concerned the *compas* who had been wounded while imprisoned at Ilopango.

The government had rejected the just demand for a general amnesty. In December 1984, as a result of the conference held on human rights, the committees of relatives of the political prisoners presented to the Legislative Assembly a proposal for an amnesty law. Throughout 1985 they continued to demand the approval of their proposal. The parliamentarians refused even to meet with them. The political prisoners themselves went on a hunger strike to increase the pressure around this issue. All those efforts proved fruitless. In his speech before the General Assembly at the UN, Duarte promised an amnesty, although the measures that the government had taken to improve the administration of justice had been purely cosmetic.

As I stared at the ceiling of my cell I wondered how many prisoners were there with me at that moment, under the same roof. Maybe some of them were people I loved, my friends.

By that time I was steeled enough to be able to watch the other prisoners paraded in front of me. In the beginning I couldn't bear it. Seeing Doroteo had been a horrible experience. When I saw Commander Hugo and Octavio it was August 20, and it filled me with sadness. I had already spent 125 days behind bars. It was the third anniversary of the Calabozo massacre.

On that day the Atlacatl battalion had murdered more than 200 women, children, and older people. I had felt so impotent! So much blood! Not too long before my capture, we had found a holy medal near that river which had probably belonged to one of the grandmothers murdered there. On December 15, 1984, the battalion had attacked our field hospital at El Salitre, near Tortuguero, in San Vicente. They took fourteen horses and all the medicines. Luckily, the seventeen wounded *compas* showed great courage and daring, and were able to get through the lines without casualties. The army was only able to capture civilians.

We had a mule named Sonia, which we used to carry the hospital equipment. She was a gorgeous mule. She had belonged to a big landowner named Juan Wright, but we had requisitioned her some time before. The soldiers from the battalion forced into sacks some of the people who had been captured and placed them in front of the mule's legs so she would kick them. She wouldn't do it. Sonia proved she had more humanity than those soldiers.

• Chapter 41 •

I was lost in my thoughts when I saw Octavio go by. He was a member of the Communist Party. He was being brought back from interrogation. He did not see me that time. A short while later I was further surprised to see Commander Hugo, second in command in the Communist Party, being taken to Cell 19. I immediately asked the jailer to take him some cookies from me.

When he was led out on his way to the interrogation cubicles I was standing close to the bars and he came up. He squeezed my hands. His eyes shone with warmth, though he looked thin and exhausted. He told me he was glad to see me, and said they had been very concerned about me.

I was very upset and barely able to smile. "When were you captured?" I asked.

"August 9," he said, holding on to my hands, in front of the guards and the jailers.

"You're going to get out of here. Just show them you've got guts," I said to him.

"We're showing them, *compañera*. We've already won."

He left, still smiling at me, not wanting to leave. They blindfolded him and took him to the interrogation room. Octavio had been led there only minutes before. I became very anxious knowing he still had several days of interrogation left. I knew Hugo was unbreakable. We had met in 1982, in the city. I got to know him through our frequent work meetings. He was very capable and very unassuming. I admired him. I saw him again a week later, only this time he was going to meet with the Red Cross. When he came back from the interview, I called him and he came over to my cell.

"When are you going to Mariona?"

"They don't want to transfer me," he said.

"Did you know that they assassinated Doroteo Gómez Arias here on August 9?"

"No, I didn't know," he answered with great concern.

The detective shouted: "Hurry up!"

He turned around and was blindfolded. It was the last time I saw him before we were freed on October 25, when we were able to embrace again. I found out later that he had been taken to Mariona three days after our conversation, and that the regime had tried to blackmail him and break his morale. They had even taken the traitor Miguel Castellanos to see him to try to persuade him to capitulate.

Octavio was taken to a cell on August 29 and moved to Mariona on September 2. I had met him in Morazán. We communicated with hand signals during the four days that he was in the cell near mine.

Once again my mind was a muddle. I sensed the beginnings of a lot of threads, but with no ends. One morning, when I went out to get some sun, I had heard a heated discussion taking place among the detectives, somewhere on the upper floors where the interrogation rooms were. There was a great commotion and talk about the capture of members of the PRTC who had participated in the actions at the Zona Rosa. The day before, three alleged members of the *Mardoqueo Cruz* commandos had been on radio and television taking responsibility for the action. The following night Revelo came by my cell. He always came on special occasions to watch my reactions, to observe me.

They put together an artist's sketch of the supposed commando leaders. They commented on how productive it had been to offer the U.S.$100,000 reward for information on those wanted.

August was coming to a close. The guerrillas had caused 672 army casualties in that month. I was very pleased. The war was progressing. The next day would see the beginning of September.

September is my favorite month. I don't know why, but it's been my favorite time since I was little. Perhaps because it is a month of contrasts, when the last of the rains depart and the temperature becomes variable. The days are either beautiful blue sky days, or very cloudy. I had never expected to see sunny days again. The sun would have to work very hard to cut through the walls of my cell and kill the dampness that permeated everything. I seemed to catch a cold every month. I was concerned about the loss of hair, though I had lots of hair. The doctor explained it was due to stress.

• Chapter 42 •

The last time I saw Doroteo Gómez Arias alive was in prison on August 8. I was really glad to see him again; he had greeted me four days before as he was leaving the interrogations cubicle. I had not known he was there and was so taken aback I could not respond. I was very moved, but felt the detective's watchful eye. It was a sad and painful encounter. His lips were cut and bloody. They had kidnapped him, beat him, cut his mouth. He looked so different from the last time I saw him, but he still managed to smile. The jailer took him away – for first aid, I hoped. About half an hour later he was again taken into interrogation.

We communicated by signals, making the "V" (for victory) sign with our hands. He let me know they had used the hood – a form of torture – on him. I sent him some cookies and a peach. I did not foresee at that moment what they had in store for him. I doubt that he did. About midnight, I heard them open Cell 17. They took him out. I felt unsettled and couldn't go to sleep. I thought it must be because my operation was coming up. The government got a lot of propaganda mileage out of the operation, trying to convince national and international public opinion that they respected human rights. Mine was an isolated case of political convenience for the regime, the only instance out of the hundreds of disappeared and tortured both in the legal and secret jails. Above all, it was a victory for the solidarity movement.

I was tossing and turning, between wakefulness and sleep, when I felt something at my throat. I couldn't breathe. Voices were shouting: "Are you going to talk or not?" I realized I was reliving my interrogation.

I started to smoke. I had recently taken up the habit again. I could let my loneliness and anxiety rise with the smoke, be absorbed by the cigarette. Smoking helped to pass the time until morning came. One never had to wait for the dark, it happened inevitably. I had to get some rest, but I wasn't sleepy. I couldn't stop thinking of the man, my comrade, I heard crying yesterday. They were punching him over and over. I could hear screams from some of the cells. Could it be someone was trying to get out? Running away, trying to escape all this? It was business as usual for the torturers!

The next day, almost at noon, Drs. Bottari and Muheim and Kurt Zeller of the International Red Cross came, together with Sandra Brin, Christine Courtright, and Dr. Sanchez of Medical Aid for El Salvador. Mike Farrell, the actor, also came as a representative of Amnesty International. They brought greetings from many people in the United States and other countries. It made me very happy.

Lieutenant Esquivel came with them. What an irony! When they arrived for the first time on May 22, and they weren't allowed to operate on me, he had also been there. How time had flown! "Nidia, we're going to operate tonight," they said.

That afternoon, Kurt Zeller brought a lot of things sent by my family. About 6:30 in the evening they put me in a van, together with four guards. There was another van and a vehicle with polarized glass in front of us, and one more behind. There were also two patrol cars. Lieutenant Serpas was in the vehicle with me. It was a big event! The clinic was located near the Shrine of the Sacred Heart. They militarized all the surrounding areas. The clinic itself was full of police. Major López Dávila and Dr. Col. Julio César Bottari. Dr. Sanchez had already arrived. Lieutenant Esquivel and Dr. Muheim were in the operating room as observers. They began the operation.

In the middle of it, the lights went out, but this didn't cause major problems. What a coincidence! Maybe it's a sabotage action by the *compas*, I thought. It was over in about three hours. I longed to be able to write and carry my weapons again.

I couldn't take either local anaesthetic or the tourniquet. After giving birth, this was the worst pain I had ever felt. My eyes welled up, but since I was in front of my adversaries, I couldn't cry.

> Let nothing demoralize me
> let nothing exasperate me,
> a guerrilla fighter's like a bull
> in the midst of a raging storm.

They were all taken aback. I was singing to my swallow, as I had done during interrogation.

Thanks to life
which has given me so much...

When we returned to the police headquarters, there was quite a commotion. Something had happened. There were many new prisoners. Each cell now held anywhere from fifteen to twenty new detainees. Several officers came up to see me. When they left, one of the detectives told me that someone had hanged himself there that day.

"What? What did he look like?"

"Tall...with a beard..."

"Who was it?"

It really hadn't occurred to me, but the next morning, August 10, I heard the news: "Doctor Doroteo Gómez Arias was found hanged in one of the cells at the National Police..." I could scarcely believe it. They had killed Doroteo while I was in surgery!

Revelo walked by and asked how I was.

"How do you expect me to be? You bastards killed Doroteo Gómez Arias!"

"No. He hanged himself."

López Dávila echoed, "Yes, he hanged himself."

"Doroteo loved his son very much," Serpas said.

So they had used the child as a weapon!

"I went to school with him," Revelo commented.

"I know he would never think about committing suicide. He was OK when I saw him and I know he had great strength of character," I said.

"Did you know him?"

"Yes, I knew him. And I know you have murdered him," I screamed as loud as I could.

"No!"

I asked the jailers, but they all had the same line: "He hanged himself," "he did it himself." They all repeated the same lie.

I remembered Chalatenango, the propaganda meeting where we shared the work of disseminating revolutionary ideas...and then how we had marched in column formation to La Palma, to the negotiations. He used to wear a big hat...His face was so serene and his embrace so warm when we said good-bye in 1984. He was so unassuming, a great revolutionary poet, an attorney at the service of the workers. His peasant figure was made more striking by his tanned features. And that contagious laugh!

I couldn't sleep, I couldn't take it any more. I had to cry! Why didn't that guard move out of the window? They hadn't been observing me since they increased my isolation. I had to cry, I couldn't absorb his death. I started crying quietly, then sobbing...I couldn't help it. The other prisoners asked me what was the matter. The guards came in, then the nurse. "Take this tranquilizer!"

"Leave me alone!" I yelled. I could not forgive those who were responsible for Doroteo's death, those who murdered him were the same ones responsible for driving others to madness, for having ruined the minds of the planters of Otomil (the God of Corn), the peasants of El Salvador. How could I forgive those who had destroyed all human tranquility with their terror? Those who planned the use of "the hood" in their torture chambers, as they put it on Doroteo? How to forgive those who kidnap, disappear, and massacre? Those who interrupted Doroteo's fevered sleep and yelled that he would rot there forever? Those who had left so many without husbands, mothers, children...How could they be forgiven? This constant horror ran deep through my veins...

That afternoon I refused to be interviewed by Gerardo Chevallier, presidential information secretary. He wanted to make public opinion believe that Duarte respected human rights and the Geneva Accords, and that he was implementing the agreement for humanization of the conflict.

That same day, the Medical Aid doctors gave a press conference, where they denounced Duarte's intransigence in not allowinwing my operation when it had been necessary, right after my capture. It was in response to this intransigence that the FMLN had two meetings with representatives of the government in order to negotiate the authorization for the operation.

Two days later, CBS came to ask me to address North Americans about my operation and the death of Doroteo Gómez Arias. I accepted and took advantage of the opportunity to denounce his assassination. The CBS reporters had first arrived in July and conducted a long interview. Clips from the interview were used by the military's press office to announce my operation. I never heard what the reaction was in the United States.

Part Six

Freedom and a new battlefront

• Chapter 43 •

I received a beautiful Larousse dictionary from the archbishop's office which the representative of the Legal Aid office brought for me. He said he did not know why the rest of my family had gone to Sweden, however my sister explained in a letter that they had continued to suffer persecution.

It had been 146 days. It was now September 10. One of the guards casually remarked he thought I'd be leaving that day.

"To go where?" I replied.

"Free!"

"I don't believe it!"

"Yes, they've kidnapped Duarte's daughter, Inés, to exchange for you."

Inés, for me? Surely this must be some new rumor! I turned on the radio and heard the sensational news of the capture carried out by a guerrilla unit. That afternoon Inés Duarte had been kidnapped and her bodyguard executed. Aside from being the President's daughter, Inés was a Christian Democratic party official and the manager of "Liberty Radio," a station owned by the Duarte family and financed with U.S. aid. The kidnap was one of the most successful operations of the urban front in recent times.

Later I learnt that initially the plan was to have been carried out on September 8. All the preparations were in place but she never showed up. So the operation was postponed. This was rather complicated, given the fact that it entailed moving about the capital of a country at war, a city which had about 25,000 soldiers readied for its protection and defense.

The New San Salvador University was located in a triangle of government buildings with the High Command of the Armed Forces some 1,200 meters away and the Military Hospital 800 to 1,000 meters. Also nearby was another military building. Avenue

49 was a busy thoroughfare with a lot of traffic.

The commando unit had to be ready to contend with the security system set up to protect Inés Duarte. Sometimes she was guarded by as many as four bodyguards, who moved about in two or three vehicles. So to have set the operation up, only to dismantle it, and then set it up again required significant organizational and conspiratorial capacity, as well as considerable calm and ability on the part of the cadre involved. After receiving the orders for the operation, the *Pedro Pablo Castillo* guerrilla unit had two weeks within which to carry it out. This required maximum effort in a short period of time. The objective was to create a way to apply a great deal of pressure on the government and the Military High Command, in order to save the lives of *compañeros* who were under threat of being killed. It was an operation that had to be completed exactly to plan if it were to be successful.

The people in charge of the operation planned very carefully and in great detail. It was important to guarantee that Inés would not be hurt or wounded – how different from the treatment that Janeth had received! It was also necessary to minimize any risks to the safety of the unit that would carry out the operation.

On September 10 Inés appeared with two bodyguards, who were traveling in another vehicle. There was some confusion when she showed up in a car that had not been previously identified, her mother's car. But they were able to deal with this surprise and proceed. The other unforeseen element was the presence of her friend Cecilia, who remained with Inés throughout the time she was held by the FMLN. Those in charge of the operation decided to hold her as well because there was a chance that she, too, might have political connections. It turned out, however, she did not.

The action took just over a minute. Above all, the plan required precision and speed in order to keep the advantage over the government forces.

The circumstances of the action were rather complicated. About 200 meters away there was an army convoy with several trucks filled with soldiers. Why they were there was not clear. They simply left when the shooting started. The rest of the military in that zone never got the chance to react. At the start an ex-colonel intervened. He had been linked to stolen vehicles and had been dismissed from the Armed Forces. He was then a student at the university. All he did was shoot, but when the guerrillas responded, he fled. Afterwards, he went back to help the security guards. But this was apparently enough to win him back his military status.

Once she had been captured, Inés was transported to a safe area. The General Command of the FMLN had assigned several *compas* to accompany and protect her. Sixteen minutes after the action was carried out, she was already out of reach of the military. They closed off the capital and brought in troops by helicopter to prevent her removal; but it was too late.

Around that time I had stopped going outside in protest against the intransigence of the Military High Command in refusing to allow my transfer to the women's jail. I was fed up with being there. I had to leave any way I could. As a last resort I intended to go on a hunger strike, which I wanted to coordinate with the political prisoners' organization. I could no longer remain passive. If, as the judge had told me, I was to be taken to the Western Prison Center, I would start my strike.

After the kidnap, the police continued to speculate about my release. They told me that I would really leave this time, that the action had been carried out for my freedom and that I would be exchanged. At that point the FMLN had not yet taken responsibility for the operation. Duarte began to show his personal interest in seeing my case resolved. The ruling class sectors expressed their sympathy with him in his pain as a father, but at the same time insisted that he should not bend to the insurgents.

When the *Pedro Pablo Castillo* commando unit of the FMLN acknowledged its responsibility, I understood the situation more clearly. But it really wasn't until October that I began to believe that the demands for the freedom of thirty-four imprisoned *compañeros* – some of whom had been listed as disappeared for as long as five years – could be fulfilled.[1] I was among those listed. Later the release of twenty-nine labor and trade union leaders, who had been illegally detained during July and August of that

---

1. The government failed to hand over the nine disappeared who had been listed, thereby confirming the death of Janeth Samour.

year, was also added to the list of demands.[1] At the same time, the FMLN was still holding twenty-three mayors and municipal officials for their role in implementing the national counter-insurgency plan. The FMLN offered their freedom if the government allowed the evacuation of ninety-six wounded war victims.

Days passed and everyone still talked about the fact that I was to be freed. But I didn't want to raise my hopes as I didn't think the regime would accept our demands. I kept asking the representatives from the human rights organizations if they knew anything and they always said they didn't. It wasn't that I didn't believe that I would one day be free to go back to whatever front of the struggle was assigned me, but I knew there were other important leaders, like Commander Hugo, who were still in prison. Furthermore, the negotiations could fail, since the government was weakened by a critical period of in-fighting among the different sectors of power in El Salvador, a crisis exacerbated by the kidnap.

The negotiations between Duarte and the FMLN became more clearly defined after a month. We forwarded to him a series of communiqués, presenting our demands for the exchange. The Military High Command and the U.S. Embassy did not want to give in. The ruling class and the oligarchy were also opposed. Duarte increasingly found himself in a difficult position.

Many communications were intercepted by the national and foreign press, even before our demands had been made public. Duarte and the guerrillas exchanged messages on the crowded airwaves of military communications. The radio and the press continually commented on the situation and placed me at the center of the exchange. This is how my name became known, not only within El Salvador, but internationally as well. The regime's hatred for me increased.

1. This last demand was added in the final phase of the negotiations. While it was not agreed to by the government in the short term, all had been released by the time of the exchange for Major Avalos in February 1987.

• Chapter 44 •

I was euphoric. I sang aloud with joy. The latest successful action carried out by our forces on the morning of October 10 had been the best way possible to celebrate the fifth anniversary of the founding of the FMLN. In spite of all the propaganda, and the psychological warfare conducted by the government to make the people believe that our movement was now disbanded and disorganized, this action showed the FMLN's offensive capacity, and demonstrated that we now held the initiative. Our growing political-military maturity was being demonstrated daily.

The cooperation among all the different forces of our movement, combined with consistent guerrilla actions that continued to bleed the front-line troops of the army, without a doubt reflected the capacity we now had to deal the regime's military machine serious blows.

After five years of struggle the unity between the different forces within the FMLN had been strengthened, though we still acted independently to some extent. The most recent agreement between the leaders would prove to be of great strategic importance, just like the announcer on the radio YSKL had observed. A new stage in the development of the revolutionary movement was beginning which would move toward the construction of the unified party – one of our greatest dreams.

The October 10 attack on the Armed Forces' Military Training Center, a garrison located a couple of kilometers from La Union Port, in the rear-guard zone of government-held territory, also demonstrated that the support of our people continued to be the basis for our victories. This attack exploded in the midst of the negotiations for the liberation of Inés Duarte.

The military training center is a key part of the army. It was founded in 1984, when they closed the Regional Center for Military Training in Puerto Castillo, Honduras. Elite battalions such as the Atonal and the Arce were trained there under the direction of the U.S. advisers. At the center, it was said, there were more than 1,800 soldiers stationed, including troops from the Arce, Jiboa, First Brigade, and others. The group of ten U.S. advisers was not there during the attack; neither was Colonel Cerna Flores. They were lucky, given that the primary objective of the attack had been either their annihilation or their capture.

The operation was led by the Commanders Jorge Meléndez (Jonas) of the Revolutionary People's Army (ERP), and Mario Alberto Mijango. We inflicted about 272 casualties, among them many cadets who were part of the instruction troops. The barracks were either partially or totally destroyed. We retrieved military equipment which brandished the emblem of the United States Army.

It was too bad the advisers were not there; our plan was meant to deal the Yankees a blow! We were not going to wait until they had a massive number of troops here to begin fighting them. Just as the action of the Zona Rosa demonstrated, we had decided to take our fire anywhere and everywhere. There could not be a safe quarter anywhere in El Salvador for those who trample our sovereignty. Nor could there be any safe place for the Yankee who captured me.

My thoughts were interrupted by the detective's voice saying, "You're a bunch of assassins! All the soldiers were asleep when you attacked. This was a cowardly act of desperation on your part."

"What do you mean 'cowardice'! This is a war, and yours is an army which works day and night, in the sun and rain, to destroy us. But more than anything, it works against the defenseless civilian population. Now, *that's* cowardice. We don't want to kill soldiers; they're the victims of a policy of intervention. We don't want those advisers here; we don't want to have to fight them, either. We believe that they, too, or at least some of them, are victims of Reagan's policy."

"You say that you want an end to the war. How? By killing?" he responded.

"Not at all! We're not in favor of continuing the bloodshed, much less at this time when there's an increasing danger of foreign intervention. Every day more and more Salvadorans, including you, are becoming more conscious of what this situation really means. Even the troops are recognizing this."

"Sure! It's you, with your actions, who are provoking it."

"No, we're not provoking it. Everyone knows that we have made several efforts to search for a political solution. You can't break us by threatening us with U.S. intervention. They cannot continue to trample upon our nation. Of course, there's always the possibility of our military victory over you — we've demonstrated our capacity to do that. I repeat, we don't want U.S. intervention. But we must be prepared for it in case it happens."

He said nothing more; he turned around and stood at the end of the passageway with his arms folded, trying to appear calm. He hung his head as if he was tormented. I almost pitied him.

The attack had been one of many actions during a period of increased FMLN activity: there was a joint operation taking place across the country against the electrical power system; an indefinite national transportation stoppage was then into its seventh day; there were regular attacks against military positions in different towns; and the FMLN was causing hundreds of casualties in the front lines of the army.

On the other hand, Duarte found himself in an even more difficult situation after the capture of his daughter. His conflict with the army had sharpened, since the army commanders at the front line did not want to negotiate for Inés, especially after they had been dealt such a major blow.

I heard radios blaring throughout the prison. It seemed everyone was continually listening to the news. Helicopters regularly flew overhead. From inside the prison you could sense the regime's feeling of defeat.

I wanted to see how Serpas and Revelo were taking the situation, but they didn't come near my cell any more. They enjoyed trying to confuse or demoralize me when things were not going so well for our movement. But after the kidnap of Inés they didn't even walk past my cell.

• Chapter 45 •

Around that time a character named Adolfo Vásquez Becker came to interview me. He was from the Guatemala News Agency. It was through him that I confirmed the existence of the list of thirty-four prisoners to be freed. He wanted to get to know me and learn more of my involvement. Some Italians from a government commission had just been to see me. They were with Serpas, coming out of one of the cells. They took my picture from the other side of the bars and asked what I thought of the events surrounding Inés Duarte.

"It's inevitable in the context of war. Our people have already suffered the disappearance and capture of tens of thousands. Why is this case so special? Such events have been daily occurrences in the life of this country for years, and now, because we decide to seek justice, everyone is shaken. There's an uproar just because she is the President's daughter. How about all the other human beings that are made to disappear by the regime? Who takes an interest in them?" was my reply.

"Do you know who's holding Inés Duarte?"

"How am I going to know? Can't you see I'm in prison and incommunicado? You on the outside are the ones who should have more information."

They turned around and left.

Hope was now growing in hundreds of families that they might once again see the loved ones whom the government held as political prisoners. Demonstrations by the relatives of the disappeared, the assassinated, and the political prisoners were on the rise. All the popular and human rights organizations had understood that it was an opportune moment to demand freedom for the political prisoners and a clarification of the fate of the disappeared. Punishment was demanded for those guilty of so many crimes. Ads on the radio and in the press demanding justice became more numerous.

The campaign known as "Stop the terror, torture, and disappearances in the jails of the Duarte dictatorship" was aimed precisely at confronting the systematic violation of individual and collective human rights in El Salvador. Repression had increased 400-fold under Duarte.

Many international organizations had documented the tortures, assassinations, and disappearances practised by the Armed Forces of El Salvador. There was no respect for fundamental human rights, nor for the Geneva Accords. The FMLN's actions won the support of the people. They had the political and military capacity to demand and ensure respect for the rights of its combatants and members and for the rights of the people.

Beginning in 1981 we had made many efforts to move towards a bilateral humanization of the conflict. The Duarte government had responded only with empty phrases as its dependence on the U.S. increased. That was why the FMLN was forced to use pressure such as the kidnapping in order to bring about a prisoner exchange.

• Chapter 46 •

My inner reflection was interrupted by the shouting of an interrogator. About two months before they had said they would no longer conduct interrogations in the cell next to mine. They continued anyway, although less frequently. This time it was a woman who was doing the interrogating. How horrible! I couldn't stand it!

"Hey, *daughter of a bitch*! Why don't you come here to interrogate me and leave the others alone? You scream at and beat the defenseless. Come over here!" I challenged.

"Calm down, Nidia," the guard said.

"I won't calm down! That woman's too much. Why doesn't she interrogate me?"

The interrogation ceased and I went to bed. But at dawn she was at it again. They had brought a lot of new people in. There was considerable tension in the air. There must have been at least eighty prisoners in interrogation.

The news program that morning had again commented on

Inés Duarte's case. In the beginning, international opinion had condemned the action, and various governments and international organizations had expressed their solidarity with Duarte. But as the reasons for the action became evident, and the violations of human rights and disrespect for international norms were made known, there was a shift in opinion. The world was moved, not just for Inés Duarte, but for the thousands of Salvadorans who were victims of the Duarte dictatorship.

"Nidia, why don't you want to go outside?" the guard asked me.

"I've already said that I will not go out in the sun again until I'm transferred to Ilopango."

That night I heard noises, as if there was a demolition going on. I could hear blows and chairs being dragged. Another interrogation? No, I realized that I was reliving my nightmares. I remembered the last press interview I had granted; I became concerned about how they would use it. They were capable of playing the tape to other prisoners. Vásquez Becker had come to probe me. I wondered why the regime wanted that interview? What will the military achieve with such an interview? Why did I agree to do it? Nidia, I told myself, you're so damn politically naive!

"I've come to ask you some personal questions," said Vásquez Becker, "because I want to write about the participation of women in the struggle. When did you begin taking part in the war? How did you become involved?"

I was so angry thinking back on it. Well, at least I didn't answer the way he wanted me to, I reassured myself. He had asked me about my personal life, my feelings, my son. What did I feel when I first took a weapon in my hands? When I fired one for the first time? How did I feel in battle? He asked about the PRTC and its origins. What had been the greatest struggle for me? Who were my best friends? Was I a Marxist? He wanted anecdotes. Ever since I saw him arrive with Serpas I knew he was one more interrogator. When he left, I knew that the information would go directly to the Military High Command. But I also knew that it wasn't going to be very useful given the time I'd been here, and also because I lied quite a bit about my life. Even so, they might confuse people and get them to believe that I talked during interrogation. They might convince them I talked by playing the tape: "Listen to Nidia, she talked! So why don't you?"

• Chapter 47 •

I learnt through a commentary on the radio that there was a video of four FMLN commanders circulating in the United States. The video showed Miguel Castellanos, "Inglés", "Grande", and myself. The tape said that the first three had collaborated, but that I had refused. I was pleased in the same way I had been glad in June, when the Zona Rosa incident took place, and they published my picture in the papers next to that of Ungo, Zamora, and Facundo. They were claiming that the "Organization of Terror" had been exposed, and that the popular movement was linked to the guerrillas. I was proud to be regarded that way. I was happy that my picture was published and my conduct was contrasted to those who had collaborated with the regime. It was the same when the oligarchy demanded that I should be tried by a military tribunal. It was important for me to know they didn't like me. Of course, as a revolutionary, a guerrilla, I had never really expected that they would.

When I joined the movement I thought I would always be underground, and that my name would never be public. Things had changed. I had joined just before my eighteenth birthday, taking a leap into a guerrilla organization after my experiences in the student movement and various Christian organizations. For a period I was only a supporter, but after 1972, when the university had been closed, I became a guerrilla member. I remember well that it was October when Paquito Montes spoke to me about becoming a full member. He handed me my weapon as a symbolic oath. October became an important month for me; a month of important decisions in my life.

When I entered the university in 1970 I immediately emerged as a student leader. I participated in the Political Student Movement. I continued some of my previous work but in a different way, working under the community action arm of the mayor's office, teaching people how to read and write in the poorer areas of the city. I became known through my activity, and with a few friends formed a philosophy study group. Miguel Castellanos was part of that group, which was led by Clara Elizabeth Ramírez.

By the time I switched from medicine to psychology, where I was later to found the Association of Psychology Students, I held a more radical view of the methods to be used in struggle. Together with some *compañeros* I had organized militant actions such as the takeover of buildings in the departments of medicine and humanities. We encouraged combative strikes. I switched fields in 1972, because studying medicine limited my time tremendously, and in addition, I had to work to support myself. The demands of political work were becoming greater. I had chosen medicine because I wanted to be a psychiatrist, so I thought that psychology would at least provide me some measure of satisfaction for my social aspirations.

I was skilled at flower arranging which I did for churches, receptions, banquets, and other ceremonies. I made all-natural arrangements, though I did make some artificial designs as well using anything from bread-crumbs to corn husks. This work enabled me to survive. I was even able to establish a bank account for our political work, with the added advantage that it was work that did not require a lot of time. I developed the skill to such an extent that I taught decoration and I owned several florist shops. The end of the year, when I was busy with Christmas decorations, was the hardest time.

My work brought me into contact with many people from different social sectors. My mother's work also broadened my social contacts. She ran a reception catering service, which included decoration. She provided a range of different price packages and therefore the customers varied greatly: there were those who worked for the government or the military, business people, even housewives. My mother also belonged to various women's reform organizations. The best known of these was the Women's League, which had fought for women's suffrage.

These broad relations allowed me access to many different places, but sometimes also placed me in what could have been compromising situations. But I was able to get by with inventiveness and conspiratorial spirit. There were periods when I did not

185

live at home, and other times when I moved between the wealthy and working class neighborhoods. I would always change my dress and my appearance according to the situation. There were also times when I combined my work in the city with going in and out of the mountains. But my work was never seriously threatened.

Practically speaking, I was able to live and move about in peace, though I could never let down my guard. The most worrying moments were the times when *compañeros* who could have known something about me were captured. This was the reason that when I was chosen to participate in the negotiations with the government, although I was very pleased, it was difficult to get used to the idea of such a public role. I paced back and forth from one end of the hut to the other, knowing that up until that moment my political activity was unknown in the legal social circles I had been a part of. After participating in the dialogue delegation it would not be easy to return.

In 1971 and 1972, almost all of my assignments were aimed at strengthening my discipline. I tested myself on things necessary to functioning in conspiratorial circles, such as how to check and counter-check, target practice, reconnaissance work, with many discussions on the revolutionary work of Lenin and Che. I was issued my first weapon around that time. I must have been looking at it strangely because the person responsible for me commented, "Don't look at it that way. I don't like them either. Guns are a necessity, that's all."

"Yes, I know there's no alternative," I answered, taking up the gun.

Later, my assignments were more complicated. I carried out military retrieval of small weapons. My political tasks included typing the stencils of a newsheet "For the proletarian cause" and recruiting sympathizers. By 1973 I was participating in more complex operations.

My friends played a very important role in my political development when I joined the movement. They were all revolutionaries or people with whom I had some common perspective. My relationship with Virginia Peña, who later became Commander Susana, was most important. She was three months older than I, and had started college one year ahead of me. We had known each other as children, but years had passed without our seeing each other. We discovered that we agreed on many things. Our friendship, which evolved during the first five years of the 1970's, I'm sure will last forever. She was a woman of exquisite sensibility. She was an artist; she played classical and folk guitar and had had voice training. Her singing style resembled that of Violeta Parra and Mercedes Sosa. She had also been instrumental in forming one of the first protest music groups, "Majucutá." She wrote a song for me, and many of the songs I sing today are hers:

> Fight, man, fight
> life awaits you
> maybe in the morning
> the sun will be at your window...

I studied Marxism and other subjects with her. She had a great analytical mind. We discussed everything under the sun. Sometimes she would stay at my house; but she never told me that she was a member of a group. I didn't tell her either, though we both knew we were part of the guerrilla movement. I didn't see her after 1975. Even though we were best friends, political interests came first and we were separated. We were living through a period of intense ideological struggle and organizational fragmentation of the movement. She was a member of the FPL and I, the PRTC. Our parting was very intense. We went to lunch at McDonald's and talked for over four hours. She had her guitar with her and so we sang, too. And in the end, it all came down to: "I'm sorry; you're my greatest friend and sister, but we don't see eye-to-eye politically, so it's best we don't see each other for the moment. Until forever. We will win."

I did not see her again until May 1984 in Chalatenango. It had been almost ten years. The unity of our forces had progressed, and this allowed the rekindling of our friendship. I had learnt in 1981 that she had been made responsible for the Guazapa front by her organization.

I had helped found the PRTC in 1975, and have played a leadership role in the organization since that time. In January 1983 we held the Third Congress of the Party, and I was reelected to the central leadership bodies, the Central Committee and the Political Committee. Given the political-military character of my work, I was given the rank of commander.

Telling this story is easy. The life of a guerrilla is not, no matter what rank or level of responsibility one has. One's attitude always has to be the same: to be conscious that one can always give more. For me the struggle has been my self-realization. My life has no meaning outside of it. My personality, my individual aspirations, and my most elementary ideas are all linked up with the struggle. I have tried to integrate the different aspects of my life; a woman is an integral being. I have always felt an ongoing revolution within me. Prison certainly revolutionized me.

When I had to go into battle or when I had to confront difficult situations — though they were situations common to all of us in the struggle — my survival instincts always rose up. Although I've had to confront the enemy in a struggle to the death, the objective has always been love and respect for human life. There have been moments of tension and indescribable emotion. I remember the first time I fired a shot I could hear my breathing and feel every beat of my heart.

In closing most of the letters from prison, I would write: "My life is the struggle for freedom; if I abandon that struggle, I will die of shame."

• Chapter 48 •

Reveille sounded. I heard the soldiers parading above me. About mid-morning Bottari, very upset, came to talk to me.

"You're leaving today, Nidia. I was expecting this to happen. I didn't believe that your *compañeros* would leave you by the wayside," he said.

"I'm not leaving. The FMLN has more important political prisoners to be freed."

"No. You're leaving. Everyone's saying so."

"Well, let them say it."

I smiled later when I heard a radio commentary on U.S. Secretary of State Shultz who had said that the FMLN was immoral. The Permanent Council of the Organization of American States had asked for the release of Inés Duarte. How could *they* speak of what is or is not moral?

I called the guard over, "Do you want me to sing you the anthem of the FMLN?"

"Why not?" he shrugged.

I looked him in the eye, and stood at attention, ordering him to follow suit.

> The FMLN
> vanguard of a people in struggle
> will guide us
> to final victory
> Brothers
> who have joined hands to do battle
> let's move the revolution forward...

The common prisoners got up and went to the bars to hear me sing. He looked back at me defiantly. I sang the entire hymn as he stood there watching.

I was lying down, looking at my pictures again. I had moved them right by my bed now, so only I could look at and enjoy them. There was the butterfly, the ballerina, the woman on horseback with her hat on; this last one reminded me more than ever of Arlen Siu Guazapa. There was Jesse Jackson breaking his chains — a symbol of rebellion. And the children's choir...They reminded me of my son. The picture with landscapes that look liked laby-rinths, seemed dialectical. I had a photo of a demonstration in Spain where they were burning the U.S. flag; another of the ocean and seagulls. I saw nature's beauty in those pictures and photographs.

A voice interrupted my wandering, "Nidia, do you have a lemon?"

Sometimes I had lemon, garlic, and honey which I would share with the other prisoners. They often asked me for candy, and every day I would try to find a way to get someone to buy some, or some bread, sugar, and cigarettes to share with the others. This had only been recently allowed. I wished I could give them more, but there were too many of them. I shared what I could with each one and they understood. Once, one of them got angry at the fact that I enjoyed the privilege of having things bought for me and of having money. I was annoyed and told him that it was a right which the political prisoners' organization had won, and that, if he were to be transferred to Mariona, he would understand because they had a store there. I told him the money and other things were sent by my family.

One Tuesday afternoon, while I was talking as usual with the Legal Aid attorney, Dr. Roberto Girón, we began to hear shouts and blows in the interrogation room. The attorney's hair stood on end, his eyes turned wild.

"This is horrible!" he exclaimed.

"Yes, but there's nothing we can do. The Ministry of Defense is handling my case and they will not budge. I can resist as long as is necessary in here, but what they're doing to me is unfair and arbitrary. That's why I protest and refuse to go outside in the sun. It's not that they're torturing me physically, but it's so painful for me to witness others being tortured."

"But this is horrible, Nidia," he repeated.

• Chapter 49 •

The only time I had for reflection was at night. Before, in the mountains, I could let my mind wander at any time. I didn't know exactly what was going on outside the prison. I had to prepare myself – not to leave – but to stay there in jail, even indefinitely. I didn't know how much longer I would be there. I told myself not to even think of the possibility of a release because if the negotiations failed I would simply end up torturing myself. I had to get ready to face worse conditions in any eventuality – to prepare for my next step, the hunger strike. I had already been a prisoner for 182 days.

The day before Monsignor Rivera y Damas and Father Ignacio Ellacuría had met with FMLN commanders Facundo, Lucio, Rogelio, Eduardo, and Armijo in Aguacayo, Suchitoto. Monsignor Rivera y Damas delivered Duarte's counter-proposal. Up until the last minute the FMLN insisted that there must be a simultaneous exchange of Inés Duarte for the political prisoners, and of the mayors who were being held for the free passage of the war wounded.

Duarte insisted that we should first release his daughter and then delay the departure of the wounded until a later date. The Armed Forces High Command, the U.S. Embassy, and even General Galvin, chief of the U.S. Southern High Command in Panama, were stubbornly opposed to their departure.

That night I began to sing at the bars. A guard came near and asked, "Nidia, what are you going to do when you see me in the street?"

"Why?"

"Because you're leaving here soon."

"Are you sad or glad?"

"Nidia, we really don't like seeing you here. It's high time you left. You don't deserve this. But what can we do?"

One had to hear this to believe that it was really taking place. I was truly astounded. Suddenly, Bottari came in and said, "I thought I wouldn't find you here any more. You'll be leaving soon. You're going to be the first one to go."

Later a sergeant came by and returned the book *One hundred years of solitude* I'd lent him. "I learnt a lot," was his comment. He handed me a piece of paper and left. I couldn't believe my eyes when I read: "Marta or Nidia, there's something about you that I won't forget, something that's had an impact on me, since what I shared with you were my weaknesses, my misery, hatred, unpleasant moments, complaints; and you wouldn't listen to them. You have such great strength of heart..."

Many policemen and guards had been coming by lately. They always seemed in a hurry. Most of them would look at me with hatred, while others just came to take a look at me from afar, since they weren't allowed to pass that way, or stay for long. They knew I was leaving and, because I no longer went out to get sun, they weren't going to see me in the yard. I felt strange. The guard's note rattled me. It seemed they all felt that they might not see me the next time, that any day now I would be leaving. I felt they were confronting their own contradictory feelings: some felt pity, others were unhappy to see me still alive.

One of the prisoners wanted to give me a military cap. He told me that the common prisoners had given it to him, but I told them I couldn't accept. I could only use military equipment if it had been captured by our forces or under different circumstances. Some of the military men there had offered me things as well and I had turned them down.

On October 18 in the afternoon First Judge Jorge Serrano came by with the prosecutor. The attorney from Legal Aid was with them. They were scared because of the last letter I had sent them:

National Police Headquarters
September 24, 1985
Dr. Jorge Serrano
First Military Judge

On July 24 and August 11 of this year, you informed me verbally and in front of Dr. Roberto Girón that you had already authorized my transfer in conformity with the law. You told me at the time that you were already coordinating it with the Ministry of Defense. It's been sixty-three days and nothing has happened.

On May 4, the First Military Instruction Judge, Colonel Melara Vaquero, showed me written notification that, while I waited to be transferred to the prison, I would be detained here. I think that it's important that you let me know in writing of your decision to transfer me to Ilopango, so I can have a legal and historical record of said decision. Similarly, I think it's important that I be notified of the arguments or obstacles presented by those who do not want my transfer to take place.

As a protest against this arbitrary decision, I'm forced, again, to take some measures. I've already been rejecting the "special food" that I was given, and now I will refuse my hour in the sun, which I was taking daily in an exercise of my rights.

That's all for the moment.

M. Valladares M. de Lemus

"Nidia, four U.S. lawyers arrived today," Serrano said. "They are interested in your case, and in your transfer to the prison at Ilopango. You know I'm doing everything that is humanly possible. Your case has been discussed with the chiefs of staff. I've shown them your letter, but your case is being considered along with those of the others who are going to be released in a few hours."

"What I asked for in my letter was a written record that you in fact processed this case and made a decision to approve my transfer to Ilopango, but that it was others who opposed it."

"Nidia, I hope you won't take reprisals against me for this, but I can't put anything like that in writing. Please realize, it would cost me my job – or worse."

"You're afraid! That's how you all behave. That's why I don't believe in you, or your laws, and even less in your political constitution. The judicial system is corrupt. Don't worry about me, I will exhaust every recourse in order to obtain my transfer. What you ought to do is worry about moving on the trials or decisions for the more than 500 political prisoners you're holding."

"Look, Nidia, with regard to your case, I have met with the minister of defense, with López Nuila, with Samayoa, with Guerrero. I've even talked on the phone with 'Engineer' Duarte. I don't know why, but they will not allow your transfer to Ilopango. Nidia, be patient; that's what they demand. But anyway you're going to get out of here soon. Don't you see that anywhere else you'd become a target for the right wing?"

"You're afraid, but I'm not. That's not the reason that I'm not allowed to go there; it's for political reasons."

He was terrified. He always seemed in that state. In July, when he came to get my deposition he was also very nervous. "Today's the day in which you have to make your declarations; I have the extrajudicial document here," he had announced.

"I refuse to declare anything," I had replied. "A prisoner of war does not make declarations. If it's a problem for you, I'll sign a note where I absolve you of all responsibility. Take note. I'm going to dictate..."

• Chapter 50 •

I wish to clarify the reason why I don't want to make or sign a declaration: Firstly, I am aware of the role each one of you plays and the reason you are here. I did not sign the extrajudicial agreement because I do not believe in your judicial procedures, nor in your laws, and because I did not agree with its contents. I did not make a declaration before the military judge because I do not believe in the present political constitution, or in the military or penal codes, nor do I believe in your decrees or your laws. I relieve you of all responsibility for my not having signed, since you said absolutely nothing either for or against doing so.

They read out my statement and I signed it. They were all standing in silence. Dr. Serrano, a small man, seemed quite shaken by my intransigence.

"Don't be so surprised," I said. "Surely it's to be expected that I will not sign or make declarations because I accept neither your arguments nor your accusations, your manipulations, distortions, and slander. The facts about my life, the origins and the development of the revolutionary path I have chosen, of my participation in the struggle, will become known — but in due course. Then my people will appreciate its worth. There are many who can testify to our lives, but for the moment they work anonymously in the cities, in the war zones, or imprisoned in your jails. My witnesses are those whose blood flows throughout the history of El Salvador. Without lies or inventions, the truth will be known. But not now, not in these circumstances. It will be made known by my people and their vanguard.

"Your so-called justice can judge me today. Should those who violate human, social, and political rights, and trample on our sovereignty, dare to judge me? That's right, gentlemen, it is the accomplices to selling out our country who want to judge me. So the unjust want to judge me? How can they? My people's sense of justice has already absolved me and I am free. You can make your judgements whenever you like."

That was three months earlier. They still had that same, frightened expression on their faces today.

Serrano tried to explain, saying, "Nidia, we have so many cases awaiting resolution. In my desk I have two folders, one concerning military offenders and the other political offenders. There are hundreds, and I can only solve one to five cases per month, so that they can be tried or freed for lack of evidence."

"Who are the military offenders?" I asked, intrigued.

"The soldiers that commit acts of insubordination. There are a lot of them in the jails."

We spoke for nearly two hours. He was a typical case of a functionary caught up in an impossible system, unable to fulfil the duties assigned to him by law.

In the negotiations over the president's daughter, the army did not stand to benefit directly, as it had at the end of the previous year. On that occasion, in return for allowing the evacuation of sixty FMLN war wounded, the army had obtained the return of eight army officers, including Major Medina Garay, who were prisoners of war being held by the FMLN. The direct beneficiary in this current swap would only be Duarte, personally. So the president had to make economic and political concessions to the army. He promised to obtain more U.S. aid for the military.

Before the FMLN action, the president and the Christian Democratic Party had very little real power. Now, with each passing day, they had even less. The United States was in a contradictory position: while they opposed negotiations, they also needed to maintain Duarte's liberal image. This involved a substantial boost to their military commitment and counter-insurgency strategy.

The FMLN, on the other hand, could only gain in political and human terms. The campaign for a cleansing of the judicial system and freedom for the political prisoners was strengthened. The mothers of our disappeared comrades would feel less alone now that the whole world joined them in denouncing a regime that hid behind a democratic facade. The struggle for individual and social rights had been reinvigorated, and the repression against the trade unions and the mass movement exposed.

I thought about the anguish of my mother. Now, perhaps, she could have some hope.

• Chapter 51 •

Between sleep and waking I tossed and turned, but couldn't sleep. I rose and began to put my books and clothes in order. I started to pace the cell. I couldn't be confident of my release. Everyone said maybe, while others assured me it would happen. The radio reported successful negotiations in Panama.

At 11 p.m. I heard a violent interrogation, with the accompanying blows, screams, insults, and complaints. I couldn't stand it and began to bang on the bars.

"Shut up! Shut up! Who is in charge here? Revelo has said to the Church that interrogations are prohibited here! Shut up!" I shouted hysterically.

I continued to bang on the bars and shout that they were violating human rights. "How can you beat a defenseless person?" I yelled.

"It's not us, Nidia, we're not torturing anyone. It's the inmates who are making a racket," was the detective's sarcastic reply.

They started to move chairs and slam doors. The detective ordered me not to shout. I answered that I had blood in my veins – not water like him. The prisoners from other cells also began to bang on the bars and ask what they were doing to me. They also shouted that the Duarte government violated human rights. I raised my voice and sang as loud as I could:

> We are dominated by pigs in costume
> with weapons and truncheons,
> to make us fear
> Left...two...three...four
> They're not stupid little pigs,
> they do have the occasional thought

The prisoners continued shouting: "Demagogues! Sons of bitches!"

...and so they give us little games
they like to see us play.
Left...two...
They're not so stupid little pigs...

The torturers banged on the door. From the other side I heard, in response to my song:

There in Cerros de San Pedro
a sergeant's woman fell down...

Shortly, there was silence, but the interrogation recommenced fifteen minutes later, this time more violently. I plugged my ears with cotton and somehow the hours passed. To revive my spirits I put on the white dress that the other women political prisoners had given me. Later, I wrote a letter to Revelo denouncing the interrogations in the cell next door.

National Police Headquarters
October 21, 1985
Colonel Rodolfo Antonio Revelo
Director of National Police

Greetings. On the basis of what seems to have been your decision not to carry out interrogations in cells adjoining Cell 20 (where I am imprisoned); I would like to inform you that during August, September, and October to date, while it is true that there have not been interrogations every day, I have heard at least twelve take place. The latest incident was last night at midnight. I became angry and shouted that it was prohibited. But they continued with the interrogation regardless.

By the way, could you please return my book *The Death of Artemio Cruz*.
That's all for the moment,

Nidia Díaz

Peter, who wrote articles in the United States about the activities of the Red Cross, arrived to take photos of me behind bars. He was accompanied by a delegate of the International Red Cross.

Some people from the Department of Immigration came around a second time. They had visited me the previous night to take down some personal details. They brought my passport for me to sign, though I never did receive it.

While bathing I remembered that one year ago we had dealt the regime a huge blow by shooting down Colonel Monterossa. Domingo Monterossa was a leading tactician in the counterinsurgency war and was responsible for massacres in El Mozote, Sumpul, Calabozo, and Aguacayo as commander of the Atlacatl battalion. He was commanding a military operation in Morazán when he announced to the national and international press that he had destroyed the rebel Radio Venceremos. After making a press statement in Joateca, he traveled by helicopter with other military chiefs, among them Herson Calito and Major José Armando Azmitia. Taking off it was hit by fire from one of our anti-aircraft units and crashed. In this way, our people were able to avenge our dead.

The Red Cross delegate came by mid-morning and told me that they would be concluding the negotiations the following day in Panama.[1] I was going to be freed, he said, and gave me a document to be signed, accepting that I would be freed by them in Salvadoran territory. I read it closely and signed without hesitating. I asked him for a pair of boots and two backpacks, one for my books and work materials and another for my clothes.

1. On October 20 the last phase of the negotiations to plan the exchange of the prisoners and the war wounded took place in Panama. At the fourteen-hour meeting were Salvador Samayoa and Mario Aguiñada of the FMLN and Rey Prendes for the government. Acting as intermediaries in the complex negotiations were Monsignor Arturo Rivera y Damas, Monsignor Gregorio Rosa Chávez and Ignacio Ellacuría.

• Chapter 52 •

My body swooned with emotion as I began to prepare my things. I was going back to the battlefront! I didn't care where, so long as I could see my *compañeros* again, and see the mountains, the rivers, the flowers, the butterflies, the blue sky which I loved, with its moon and stars — especially that bright little star I named José Alejandro. A lump of happiness, triumph, and home-sickness rose in my throat. How long would it be before I would see my son José Alejandro? I knew my physical condition would not make it easy for me to travel abroad.

When would I see him? It had been two years and two months. But what of the others who never saw their children again? How many orphaned children had the assassins left behind? And what of the indelible scars that these times would produce on such innocent lives?

I was to rejoin my comrades! I remembered the verses I had written:

Comrades of the mountain and the city
I miss you like I miss my wings
you gave me this strength and courage
that no one can break.
I shared with you the butterfly
and the flower,
the river and the mountain
the book and the rifle
the street and the union
the bird and the iguana.
But especially
I miss your love of humanity
and for me.

How many of us wait behind bars:
one, five, forty-three, one hundred and fifteen,
two hundred and one, three hundred and fifteen,

four hundred and fifty-five...
who knows?
There are so many
who have experienced this captivity,
to emerge with their ravaged faces,
sharing with me the pain,
the iron bars, the humidity.

How many times have we looked beyond the wall
to the world we forged,
wanting to break the chains,
longing to be part of the struggle
once more alongside you.
Even from within these four silent walls,
we sense the future
here with you,
we share the natural beauty of our land,
the song, and our victory,
the generous and helping hand
of the people.

All those memories, glimpsed in the darkness –
a hand tightening on a rifle,
silent crying behind the bars,
a lover's kiss,
a child at the breast.

I was going to see the *compañeros* again! I went through my things, seeing what I could give away to all the other prisoners. Each had asked for a keepsake. Even the warders and detectives had asked me to leave them something. To the prisoners I had given towels, socks, T-shirts, and pens. When I could I gave the women dresses and even more personal items, as sometimes fear brought on menstruation. So I contrived ways of getting sanitary pads to them, often denied by the guards to cause humiliation.

My thoughts were violently interrupted by shouts. It was the torturers at work yet again. The interrogation became increasingly violent. All night and into the early morning I heard voices. Even the closeness of my freedom would not allow me to shut my mind to what was happening behind those unyielding bars and that wall. Nor could I forget the disappeared whose memories are always with us, but whose whereabouts we will never know.

• Chapter 53 •

I heard the reveille and the parade at dawn for the last time. I slowly ran my eyes over the cell counting, as I had done so many times before, the bricks and the thirty-two bars. There was my signature on the wall, waiting in the silence alongside so many others. Cold water ran deliciously down my body and I observed each drop. From now on there would be no more imprisoned drops falling on me.

"Good morning, Nidia. You leave today," said Revelo. He startled me. It was very early, and he hadn't come by in over a month. He looked impeccable in his uniform. "Are your things ready?"

"Yes, they are."

"Well, you have to be ready. Here, I'm returning the book you lent me." It was *The Death of Artemio Cruz*, by Carlos Fuentes. Although I had written him a note requesting its return, I had changed my mind. The book might do him some good.

"You can keep it. Share it with some of the other officers," I said.

People were bustling about, crowding the whole area. All the guards wanted to be on duty when I left. I was nervous and tried to calm myself a little. The tension was palpable. The two nurses who had been kind to me came in. They were crying, which surprised me. "You're going, Nidia. We're so happy for you," they said.

Kurt Zeller appeared with two suitcases.

"But I didn't ask for suitcases – I wanted backpacks. How am I going to carry these in the mountains? And my boots?"

"Plans have changed. You're not going to the mountains. You're going abroad."

"Abroad?" Again my mind was overwhelmed. I had prepared

myself the night before to go to the war zones. Now it turned out I was going abroad.

"And where am I going?"

"We don't know!"

"Well I should leave all the books and things for the prisoners' association. Wait a minute, I'll put it all together," I said.

"We have to go down right now," said Kurt.

There were two officers with a photographer outside the cell. López Dávila was also there. They walked beside me.

"Goodbye, Nidia! Goodbye, Nidia!" the other prisoners, crowding at the bars, shouted after me. I went up to the gates to say goodbye. I shook their hands, one by one. I felt I was about to cry, but tried to hold it back as I said, "Remember we are still beside you. We won't forget you. Goodbye!"

As I walked down the photographer took my picture at every step. The prison guards, the construction workers, the administrators, even the common criminals, all lined up to watch me go.

"Goodbye, Nidia!"

"You're grinning from ear to ear, Nidia," remarked López Dávila.

"Why not? I'm so happy. You can't imagine *how* happy I feel."

We filed into Serpas's office, where amongst all the cameras, there were many other people: diplomatic personnel from Panama, Mexico and Spain; María Julia from the archbishop's office; and Kurt Zeller. But suddenly in that crowd of people I saw Graciela's shining eyes. She embraced me. What a sister she was to me! How many years had it been since I saw her? I wondered if she had any idea how much the example of her conduct in jail as a leader of the political prisoners' organization had helped me.

López Dávila read the act of freedom. Why didn't Revelo or Serpas read it? Obviously it had to be the head of intelligence to read and sign the document. It was 9:30 in the morning – one of the greatest moments in my life.

• Chapter 54 •

On leaving the room, I encountered the officials gathered in a semicircle, waiting to take leave of the diplomats. I could not avoid shaking hands with them. When Revelo shook my hand, his emotions took hold of him and he embraced me, saying "I wish you luck."

"Why did you let *that* animal embrace you?" Graciela asked crossly.

"Why not, it doesn't take anything away from me," I answered.

In the carpark Graciela surprised everyone by shouting in that militant voice of hers: "Long live the General Command of the FMLN!"

"Viva!" I responded.

"Long live the freedom of Commander Nidia Díaz!"

"Viva!"

The surprises were not yet over. I had to climb aboard an armored car. As I took my last view of the national police barracks I vowed silently to leave my nightmare there in those tall grey buildings.

As the armored car left the police barracks I saw the streets of San Salvador. What an experience! I felt like a bird whose wings had been sleeping. Graciela was beside me, her large eyes beaming with happiness. We had discussed a thousand topics and taught each other so many things. María Julia and the Panamanian representative, Didio Sosa, watched us. The situation overwhelmed me.

We traveled towards the Mariona jail through the muddy, rocky streets of Mejicanos. The twenty-two liberated prisoners, including myself, would meet there to be handed over to the diplomatic corps, the International Red Cross, the Church, and the rector of the Central American University, Ignacio Ellacuría. There were hundreds of journalists outside. As it was visiting day, the prisoners' families were there as well, but were not allowed to enter. They took me to a room where there were journalists from the government radio and television.

All of the *compañeros* who were going to be liberated entered two by two. We embraced amongst tears and joyful greetings. I had never realized that we loved one another so much. Some of them I had never met, yet I felt I knew them. They presented me with a belt – the same one they had been forbidden to give me previously – along with a bracelet and ring that they had made for me.

I was asked by Julio Samayoa, minister of justice, and Vice-President Rodolfo Castillo Claramount to sign a document. My signature meant my freedom. At this moment Commander Hugo, using the communication equipment of the International Red Cross, advised the FMLN that we were all now free and ready to depart. The *compas* gathered in the parking lot. A truck with the banner of the Red Cross was waiting for them there. The diplomats, the representatives of the Church, and other observers would go with them. More than fifteen countries and international organizations[1] participated in the exchange and delivery of the prisoners.

Before leaving the office a young man approached me carrying a photo of himself beside a leader of the prisoners' group, under an FMLN flag. He asked me whether I would write a few lines and autograph it. I assumed he was a comrade, but it turned out he was one the jail's superintendents. That annoyed me, but it was too late. I never saw him again, he left so quickly. Maybe he was looking to protect his future.

I don't remember how I came to be given a microphone, but I began to address the crowd. "Salvadorans," I said, "thanks for your confidence and your struggle. I am happy about this victory but sad that there are still comrades whose present circumstances are unknown. Please remember the disappeared and the civilians who have been killed. The murderers go free. There are more than 500 political prisoners in our country's jails. The struggle must continue so that all those people can be freed..."

At about the same time in the mountains, the *compañeros* gave a microphone to Inés Duarte who said, "The people of the FMLN fight with conviction and high morale. By living with

---

1. Those countries which assisted in the exchange were Sweden, Switzerland, Spain, France, Germany, Italy, Argentina, Costa Rica, Panama, Peru, Colombia and Mexico.

them, I have seen how they live, their unity, their solidarity, and I have spoken with them...I confess that I was afraid, and the young people in charge of our security gave us a certain impression...However, I now have a different view of the struggle and the environment in which it has developed."

I realised Didio Sosa had left and was taking photos of the *compañeros* who had been freed and were climbing on to the truck. Although I had not been given permission to accompany them, I ran out shouting, "Long live the General Command of the FMLN! Long live our freedom! United in combat...until final victory!"

"Revolution or death, we will win!" they answered.

The truck started out alone, without an escort. In fact, they had refused to accept the presence of a military vehicle accompanying them, since it could have provided the army with an opportunity to carry out a provocation. Meanwhile, in Tenancingo, Inés Duarte was handed over unharmed to Monsignor Rivera. She was later taken to Santa Cruz Michapa from where she was brought by helicopter to the High Command of the Armed Forces.

Commanders Facundo Guardado and Lucio of the FMLN, the International Red Cross, Monsignor Rivera y Damas, and the ambassadors of France, Panama and others, awaited our *compañeros* in Tenancingo. Simultaneously, in twelve different zones, twenty-three mayors were handed over in return for the evacuation of 101 of our wounded. The campaign "No More Terror..." was thus concluded.

We climbed into the Panamanian embassy car and Didio took leave of everyone. Father Ellacuría,[1] Samayoa, Castillo Claramount, and others were nearby. I shook hands and embraced those who remained, amidst exclamations of "Good luck, Nidia! Look after yourself! Hope things go well."

---

1. Father Ignacio Ellacuría played an important intermediary role in this negotiation process from the end of September, along with Monsignor Rivera y Damas. Even though the FMLN had not publicly acknowledged it had captured Inés Duarte at the time, it had already informed the government. The government established direct but unofficial contact from that point on.

• Chapter 55 •

I spent all day in the Panamanian ambassador's residence, along with the freed prisoners William and Marcelino, who were also going abroad for health reasons. We were in high spirits, we ate well, and the conversation flowed easily. That night we left the embassy. A series of spotlights accompanied us as far as the entrance to the Comalapa airport. We held up two fingers to signal "V" for victory. They parked almost alongside the plane, but I was unable to board because of the enormous number of journalists blocking my path. They asked a torrent of questions, but I was not able to reply, according to the agreement reached in Panama. However, I did finally respond to a few questions.

"Commander Nidia, what will you do now?"

"Continue to struggle as I have done in the past, only better," I replied.

"Will you return?"

"If the FMLN General Command so orders, I will return."

"When will that be?"

"Soon!"

Journalists anxiously took me by the arm: How did I feel? What did I think of the Duarte government? How had the president acted in the end?

There were many Panamanian journalists on the plane, so the questions began again, with tape recorders and cameras set in motion. I was both stunned and nervous. I had to be careful. I had had no official briefing from the FMLN as to what comments I could make. Everyone wanted to be photographed alongside me, even the photographer. The situation was all so completely new.

Also in the plane was Julio Lodoño, the Columbian ambassador in Panama, whom I had met during the negotiations at La Palma.

Just traveling with the *compañeros* who had been crippled in the war gave me great satisfaction. They had come from all over. Their trip to board the plane was made more difficult by their delicate condition. The army tried to block the exit of two groups, from Chalatenango and Usulután. This was a violation of the Panama pact, which had established that neither side should carry out military operations while the complicated exchange was taking place.[1] The army had set up ambushes and our scout forces had responded, causing three casualties. It had been a severe blow for the Armed Forces when the case became known and they had to accept responsibility for the violation.

The *compas* arrived exhausted a few at a time. Some had walked along rough highways, climbing over hills, fording deep streams and crossing deserted valleys. Many had walked for two days without rest. Some of them were in a serious condition. The majority had never been in a plane before and had never confronted their enemy at such close range, and felt uneasy being defenseless, unarmed. Yet every face beamed victory and contentment. I watched them arrive from the front seat – the mutilated angels, I thought to myself. Once in the air, they handed me a microphone.

"Welcome, *compañeros*," I began. "Today is the day of a great political and military victory. The FMLN operation 'No more terror, disappearances, torture or murder in secret jails' has been victorious. We leave our country in freedom to recover our health..." They applauded and shouted a few slogans. We spent the whole flight singing and shouting.

After landing at Panama airport, we disembarked singing the FMLN anthem. I was overwhelmed by camera flashes, questions and statements. I was under siege when *compañero* Mario Aguiñada Carranza appeared, embraced me, and on behalf of the FMLN announced that it was time to board another plane.

"Where to?" I asked.

"Cuba."

---

1. Six centers were established to receive the war wounded and a further eight centers to receive the town mayors, all as part of the complex exchange of prisoners.

• Chapter 56 •

That is how simply he put it. I felt as though a current of electricity had raced through my body.

"To Cuba?" I echoed.

I could not believe it. I had never been to Cuba. We had tried so many times to go there but there was always something else to do. Like any revolutionary, to visit Cuba was one of my greatest aspirations. They introduced me to a tall, mulato Cuban *compañero*. His expression was full of tenderness. As we boarded the plane, Cuban doctors and nurses already began to treat the most seriously injured. The expression of an FMLN representative in Cuba, Jorge Palencia, and that of the Cuban *compa* remains vivid in my mind. I gazed at both of them, but without thinking of them. I was in another world.

It was a supreme moment in my life. Thousands of memories tumbled over one another in my mind. I was reliving those events, remembering everything that had happened. But it was all too much – all so unfortunate. My capture had been so abrupt, and my release so sudden and unexpected. Everything that had happened already seemed like a nightmare in my mind. Everything that was happening seemed like a dream – a fantasy, like winning a lottery. I closed my eyes; I was in ecstasy.

The accidental and the intentional seemed so interwoven: I had to fight that last battle. I could not have died crushed like a worm. But afterwards I had no choice. Once I was captured there was nothing left but death and it seemed my destiny to be disappeared. I was revived by the love, the thought, the action, the struggle, the responsibility, and the conviction of our movement. And later? Survival. One hundred and ninety, 190 long days. Days of struggle against isolation and pressure, days of progress and regaining feeling. Sharing a smile with other prisoners, being careful even about my gestures in front of the guards. Controlling my facial expressions was a duty, for I could not allow myself to show any sign of weakness.

Now I was in the clouds, flying towards the construction of

socialism. The cruelty and taunts of the prison were left behind. That April 18, one second, one instant, could have meant the difference between life and death. One breath and everything would have been nothingness – instead of this happiness of now sailing towards victory. The path of one bullet, inaccurate or true, could have meant my becoming another name in my people's history, part of my people's memory, a slogan at a rally, "Commander Nidia Díaz, present!" Or a few months later I could have so easily disappeared without a trace, with my mother, relatives, and comrades going door to door asking for me: "This is what she looked like. Have you seen her?"

• Chapter 57 •

Now, I was free, ready to continue the struggle, no longer from the confines of the prison, the fifth war front, but wherever necessary. As I closed my eyes tightly my heart beat even faster. I felt as though I had lived through a century of experiences, that reality and fantasy, past and present, had become one. I felt as though I had only closed my eyes in the war zone for a moment, and had just woken up. That nothing happened; that there was no prison, no painful time, that I had always been here – or in the war zone. I had simply been transported from an evening on April 18 to this dawn of October 25.

But what if I had not believed in the present? If I had not had confidence in the future? If I had not understood the historical legacy left by thousands of compatriots? If my moral reserves had not been so solid – if I weakened for even an instant? I could not have lived with myself, to be looked down on by my people, by my comrades. Such a different fate! But we proved that we were made of different stuff; those like Miguel Castellanos are the sad exception. I knew I had acted as a revolutionary should. Miguel had not.

My thoughts were interrupted by a pleasant Cuban voice announcing, "We have arrived, Nidia. Time to disembark." The plane door was opened and the chill dawn air entered. "You should leave first, Nidia," he said.

"No, I'd rather go together with all the *compas*. What about them?"

"They can follow."

I was stuck there in the plane. What should I do? I made the decision. "OK, I'll leave first."

Hundreds of people with cameras applauding and shouting slogans surrounded me. Only those who have experienced such a moment can understand how it feels. I was filled with new life.

"The people, united, will never be defeated! The people united, will never be defeated! The people united, will never be defeated!"

"Revolution or death, we will win!"

Venancio was there, dear old Venancio! So were Vladimir and Silvia to welcome us as representatives of the Cuban people. I raised my hand with the "V" of victory and gave a broad smile. We embraced. We were reunited. I was amongst my comrades. The others began to leave the plane.

At that moment I not only realized that I was not alone, but something even more important – that I was never alone.

Published by Ocean Press

An encounter with Fidel

Introduction by Gabriel García Márquez

"This is the Fidel I believe I know: a man of austere ways and insatiable illusions, of cautious word and simple manners and incapable of conceiving any idea which is not out of the ordinary...he is one of the great idealists of our time and perhaps this may be his greatest virtue, although it has also been his greatest danger."

...Gabriel García Márquez

This marathon interview prepared for Italian television by Gianni Mina presents a rare insight into Fidel Castro and his views of Cuba and the world.

Castro discusses such controversial issues as human rights; Khruschev, Kennedy and the Cuban missile crisis; Gorbachev and the Soviet Union; the merits of socialism and capitalism; and US-Cuba relations in the Reagan and Bush years.

Castro reflects on his personal role in the revolution and for the first time speaks intimately of his relationship with Che Guevara.

275pp, index
ISBN paper 1 875284 21 4
ISBN cloth 1 875284 22 2

Published 1991

Published by Ocean Press

Changing the history of Africa: Angola and Namibia

Why did more than 300,000 Cubans — of all ages and professions, men and women, black and white — volunteer to help defend Angola from repeated South African invasions? Was the presence of these Cuban forces in Angola an obstacle to Namibia's independence and peace in the region? Were they a threat to U.S. security as Washington often claimed?

With contributions from Colombian writer Gabriel García Márquez, as well as Fidel Castro, Jorge Risquet, and Raúl Castro, this book helps to provide a background to the events in Southern Africa. It includes details of the battle of Cuito Cuanavale, in which South Africa was decisively defeated and which Fidel Castro has described as a turning point in the history of Africa.

Here for the first time in such depth Cuban leaders discuss Cuba's participation in Africa.

175pp plus 32pp photos, index, chronology
ISBN paper 1 875284 00 1

Published by Ocean Press

A new society
Reflections for today's world

by Che Guevara

Has socialism future? Che Guevara's perspective on the transition to a new society in the early years of the Cuban revolution as presented in this selection contributes to the discussion in the world today on the future of socialism.

Fidel Castro has said that "as a man of profound thought, Che had the exceptional opportunity during the first years of the revolution to delve into the building of socialism."

This book is the product of Che Guevara's experience as the President of the National Bank, the Minister of Industry, and as a central figure in the revolutionary government.

Introduction by Fidel Castro

234pp plus 16pp photos, index
ISBN paper 1 875284 06 0
ISBN cloth 1 875284 45 1

Published by Ocean Press

Cuban women confront the future

by Vilma Espín

How has family life in Cuba changed since the revolution? How are Cuban women confronting the discrimination and prejudices of the past? How do they see their gains and the challenges still facing them today?

Vilma Espín, in all the interviews and essays included in *Cuban women confront the future*, in a frank and informative style, makes an important contribution to the international discussion on the role women have to play in building a socialist society.

Espín is the president of the Federation of Cuban Women.

95pp
ISBN paper 1 875284 23 0